Real English *for* Hotel Staff

실무편

노 선 희

학력사항
- 세종대학교 호텔관광대학원 호텔관광경영학 전공 (호텔관광경영학 박사)
- Master's Degree in Hospitality Management, Florida International University

경력사항
- 현) 백석대학교 관광학부 교수
- ㈜호텔신라 서울, 객실부
- The Fairmont Turnberry Isle Resort & Club (Florida, USA), Rooms Division
- Hyatt Regency Pier 66 (Florida, USA), Front Office Department
- 그랜드 인터컨티넨탈 호텔 서울, 식음료부

Real English for Hotel Staff 실무편

지은이 노선희
펴낸이 정규도
펴낸곳 (주)다락원

초판 1쇄 발행 2016년 12월 7일
초판 3쇄 발행 2023년 9월 8일

편집 김태연, 조상익
디자인 박보희, 윤현주
영어감수 Michael A. Putlack

다락원 경기도 파주시 문발로 211
내용문의 (02) 736-2031 내선 550
구입문의 (02) 736-2031 내선 250~252
Fax (02) 732-2037
출판등록 1977년 9월 16일 제406-2008-000007호

Copyright ⓒ 2016 노선희

저자 및 출판사의 허락 없이 이 책의 일부 또는 전부를 무단 복제·전재·발췌할 수 없습니다. 구입 후 철회는 회사 내규에 부합하는 경우에 가능하므로 구입문의처에 문의하시기 바랍니다. 분실·파손 등에 따른 소비자 피해에 대해서는 공정거래위원회에서 고시한 소비자 분쟁 해결 기준에 따라 보상 가능합니다. 잘못된 책은 바꿔 드립니다.

ISBN 978-89-277-0920-6 18740
978-89-277-0918-3 18740 (set)

http://www.darakwon.co.kr
다락원 홈페이지를 방문하시면 상세한 출판 정보와 함께 MP3 자료 등의 다양한 어학 정보를 얻으실 수 있습니다.

Real English for Hotel Staff

실무편

노선희 저

　전 세계 국제관광객 수는 이제 한 해 10억 명이 넘으며 우리나라에도 매년 1,300만 명이 넘는 외래 관광객이 찾아오고 있습니다. 관광산업의 발전에 따라 호텔산업 분야도 끊임없이 발전을 거듭하고 있습니다. 이러한 시대에 발맞추어 호텔에서는 지원자에게 다양한 자질을 요구하고 있는데 그중에서도 영어회화 구사 능력은 채용을 결정하는 데 중요한 열쇠가 됩니다. 즉 영어로 자기 생각을 자유롭게 표현하고 의사소통을 원활하게 할 수 있는 능력은 이제 호텔리어의 필수요건이 되었습니다.

　본서는 고객이 호텔을 예약할 때부터 퇴실할 때까지 관여하는 담당 부서에 따라 순차적으로 단원을 구성하였습니다. 특히 호텔 현장 경험이 없는 예비 호텔리어에게 가장 취약한, 부서별 업무 내용을 다양하게 다루어 간접적으로나마 현장 경험을 해볼 수 있도록 하였습니다.

　본서는 대학의 호텔 및 관광 관련학과 수업교재로는 물론, 호텔 취업 준비생을 위한 독학교재로도 사용할 수 있습니다. 각 단원은 다양한 상황별 대화문과 핵심 표현을 제공하며, 호텔리어와 고객 간 상황극을 연출해볼 수 있도록 롤플레잉 코너도 수록하였습니다. 또한, 매 단원의 마지막 페이지에는 각 호텔 부서를 소개하는 글을 실었으므로 독해 연습과 더불어 호텔 업무 지식을 넓히는 기회로 활용하시기 바랍니다.

　장차 호텔리어가 될 학생들에게 본서가 유용한 지침서가 되기를 진심으로 바랍니다. 끝으로 본서의 출간을 위해 애써주신 다락원 관계자분들께 깊은 감사의 마음을 전합니다.

2016년 11월

노선희

Contents

To the Students
Plan of the Book

UNIT 1 Switchboard   p.10
- Giving Information   p.12
- Handling Guest Requests   p.15

UNIT 2 Reservations   p.22
- Taking Room Reservations   p.24
- Handling Requests After Reservations   p.28

UNIT 3 Door & Bell Desk   p.34
- Doorman Service   p.36
- Bellman Service   p.39

UNIT 4 Front Desk I (Reception)   p.46
- Check-In Service   p.48
- In-House Guest Service   p.51

UNIT 5 Front Desk II (Cashier)   p.58
- Checkout Service   p.60
- Handling Disputed Charges & Other Cashiering Services   p.64

UNIT 6 Concierge & GRO Desk   p.70
- Concierge Service   p.72
- GRO (Guest Relations Officer) Service   p.75

UNIT 7 Executive Floor   p.82
- EFL Check-In & Checkout Service   p.84
- Lounge & Meeting Room Service   p.86

UNIT 8 Housekeeping   p.92
- Making up Rooms   p.94
- Other Housekeeping Services   p.97

UNIT 9 Hotel Facilities   p.102
- At the Business Center   p.104
- At the Fitness Center   p.107

UNIT 10 Room Service   p.112
- Taking Orders for Room Service   p.114
- Delivering Room Service   p.117

UNIT 11 Restaurants & Bars   p.122
- Reserving Tables & Greeting Customers   p.124
- Taking Orders & Handling Payments   p.128

UNIT 12 Complaints & Problems   p.134
- Guest Complaints   p.136
- Guest Problems   p.141

Answer Key   p.148

Plan of the Book

Unit	Topic	Objectives	Situations
1	Switchboard	- Giving Information - Handling Guest Requests	- Giving information about transportation, hotel facilities, and hotel services - Connecting guests' calls - Making wakeup calls - Handling wrong numbers
2	Reservations	- Taking Room Reservations - Handling Requests After Reservations	- Taking room reservations, explaining cancelation policies, putting customers on the waiting list - Handling special requests - Changing, canceling, and confirming reservations
3	Door & Bell Desk	- Doorman Service - Bellman Service	- Welcoming and helping hotel guests - Valet parking and saying farewell to guests - Taking guests to their rooms - Showing guests their rooms - Handling baggage service
4	Front Desk I (Reception)	- Check-In Service - In-House Guest Service	- Check-in process - Room changes, hotel shuttle service, locked-out guests, and hotel facilities - Extending stays & providing extra beds
5	Front Desk II (Cashier)	- Checkout Service - Handling Disputed Charges & Other Cashiering Services	- Preparing for checkout, the checkout process, settling bills, and extending checkout times - Handling disputed charges, settling accounts, and exchanging money - Handling guest complaints during checkout
6	Concierge & GRO Desk	- Concierge Service - GRO (Guest Relations Officer) Service	- Recommending tourist attractions, restaurants, and shopping places - Locating lost items - Treating VIP guests - Giving information regarding hotel events and facilities
7	Executive Floor	- EFL Check-In & Checkout Service - Lounge & Meeting Room Service	- EFL check-in & checkout services - EFL lounge service - EFL meeting room service

Unit	Topic	Objectives	Situations
8	Housekeeping	- Making up Rooms - Other Housekeeping Services	- Making up rooms - Requesting rooms be made up, turndown service, and other services - Laundry service - Handling lost & found items
9	Hotel Facilities	- At the Business Center - At the Fitness Center	- Photocopy and printing services - Courier and meeting room services - Gyms, saunas, and swimming pools
10	Room Service	- Taking Orders for Room Service - Delivering Room Service	- Taking orders for breakfast - Taking orders for lunch and dinner - Checking orders & delivering room service - Handling mistakes
11	Restaurants & Bars	- Reserving Tables & Greeting Customers - Taking Orders & Handling Payments	- Taking restaurant reservations - Assigning tables to customers with reservations and walk-in customers - Serving at the bar - Taking orders, checking on diners, suggesting desserts, and handling payments
12	Complaints & Problems	- Guest Complaints - Guest Problems	- Complaints about room facilities, mischarges, and wrong rooms - Complaints about restaurant service - Problems with guests' mistakes and room temperatures

NCS 연계 단원 안내

분류체계	능력 단위 및 분류 번호	능력단위요소	연계 단원
직업기초능력 〉 의사소통능력	기초 외국어 능력 A-2-마.	외국어 듣기 일상생활의 회화 활용	Unit 1-12
12. 이용 • 숙박 • 여행 • 오락 • 스포츠 〉 03. 관광 • 레저 〉 02.숙박서비스 〉 02. 객실관리	객실 예약 접수 1203020201_13v1	객실 및 부대시설 이용정보 파악하기 고객 이력과 기호 확인하기 예약 관련 자료 작성하기 예약 변경하기	Unit 2
	체크 인(Check In) 1203020202_13v1	고객 응대하기 등록카드 작성하기 객실 키 발급 및 정보 제공하기	Unit 4

	재실 고객 관리 1203020203_13v1	고객 요청 사항 처리하기	Unit 4, 8
		객실 변경(Room Change) 하기	Unit 4
		고객 불평 접수하기	Unit 3, 12
	객실 수납 1203020204_13v1	전기(Posting)하기 환전 업무하기	Unit 5
	체크 아웃(Check Out) 1203020206_13v1	투숙객 정보 확인하기 추가 사용 내역 확인하기 최종 내역 계산하기	
		환송하기	Unit 5, 6
	하우스키핑 정비 1203020208_13v1	오더 테이킹(Order Taking) 처리하기 턴다운 서비스하기	Unit 8
	하우스키핑 관리 1203020209_13v1	호텔 습득물 처리하기(Lost and Found)	
	호텔 세탁물 관리 1203020210_13v1	고객 세탁물 접수 처리하기	
12. 이용·숙박·여행·오락·스포츠 〉 03. 관광·레저 〉 02. 숙박서비스 〉 **03. 부대시설관리**	호텔 레스토랑 서비스 1203020302_13v1	고객 예약 응대하기 고객 영접 및 환송하기 메뉴 추천 및 메뉴 주문 받기 음식 서빙하기	Unit 11
	호텔 음료 서비스 1203020303_13v1	음료 서빙하기	
	식음료 고객 관리 1203020306_13v1	고객 불평 처리하기	Unit 12
12. 이용·숙박·여행·오락·스포츠 〉 03. 관광·레저 〉 02. 숙박서비스 〉 **05. 접객서비스**	도어 데스크 1203020502_13v1	현관 환대 및 환송하기 발렛 차량 호출하기 택시 호출하기 고객 수하물 전달하기	Unit 3
	벨 데스크 1203020503_13v1	수하물 운반하기 객실 안내하기 고객의 물품 보관하기	
	컨시어지(concierge) 1203020504_13v1	요청받은 정보 제공하기 예약 대행하기 셔틀버스 관리하기 우편물 관리하기	Unit 6
	GRO(Guest Relations Officer) 1203020505_13v1	버틀러 서비스 제공하기	
	귀빈층 라운지(EFL) 1203020504_13v1	귀빈 층 라운지 고객의 체크인, 체크아웃하기 귀빈 층 라운지의 식음료 서비스하기 귀빈 층 라운지의 서비스 안내	
	비즈니스 센터 1203020504_13v1	회의실 관리하기 문서의 복사 및 제본하기	Unit 9
	고객 서비스 센터 1203020508_13v1	내·외부의 전화 연결하기 호텔 상품 안내하기	Unit 1
		객실 고객에게 주문받기	Unit 10
		웨이크 업 콜(Wake-up Call)하기	Unit 1

Unit Objectives
◇ Giving Information
◇ Handling Guest Requests

1
Switchboard

Warming Up

A Look at the picture below. Who are they? What are they doing? Share your thoughts with your partner.

B What does a telephone operator do? Check the correct boxes.

a. Handles phone calls to the hotel ☐	b. Connects calls to guest rooms ☐
c. Makes room reservations ☐	d. Takes orders from guests ☐
e. Delivers room service ☐	f. Makes wakeup calls to guests ☐
g. Gives information and directions ☐	h. Deals with requests from guests at the front desk ☐

Vocabulary Match each word or phrase with its correct definition.

1. put through
2. stay on the line
3. engaged
4. be located
5. call back
6. step out
7. last name
8. spell

a. to wait and not hang up the phone
b. to state the letters of a word in order
c. to be in a particular place
d. to connect someone to someone else on the telephone; to transfer
e. busy
f. to leave a place for a short amount of time
g. another term for a surname; a family name
h. to call again

Hotel Terminology Learn the following words and phrases used in the hotel industry.

hotel limousine	a hotel car driven by a hotel driver according to passengers' requests
house phone	a telephone mainly installed in a hotel lobby; a telephone one can use to call a hotel operator or guest rooms
operator	an employee who connects telephone calls to requested departments or guest rooms
PBX	private branch exchange; a telephone system that handles the internal and external calls of a hotel
switchboard	a place in a hotel where all the telephone calls are connected
wakeup call	a service which involves calling guests in their rooms at certain times to wake them up

Tips to Know

Spelling Alphabet

A spelling alphabet, which is often called a radio alphabet or a telephone alphabet, is a set of words used to stand for the letters of the alphabet in oral communication. When speaking on the telephone, a person can find it useful to spell a word by using the spelling alphabet. For example, to spell PARK, you could say, "**P** for Papa, **A** for Alpha, **R** for Romeo, **K** for Kilo."

| Alpha | Bravo | Charlie | Delta | Echo | Foxtrot | Golf | Hotel | India | Juliet | Kilo | Lima | Mike |
| November | Oscar | Papa | Quebec | Romeo | Sierra | Tango | Uniform | Victor | Whiskey | X-ray | Yankee | Zulu |

Conversation 1: Giving Information

A. Giving information about transportation

Operator	Thank you for calling the Emerald Hotel. This is Linda speaking. How may I assist you?[1]
Caller	Hello. How can I get to your hotel from Incheon International Airport?
Operator	You can take a taxi, an airport limousine bus, or our hotel limousine. Which one would you prefer?
Caller	This is my first business trip to Korea, and I need to stop by the COEX Center before I go to the hotel.
Operator	Well, why don't you use our limousine service?[2] We can drop you off at the COEX Center and then take your luggage to the hotel.
Caller	That's wonderful! I'm definitely going to use the limousine service then.
Operator	You can reserve it when you make a room reservation. The limousine pickup service fee is 140,000 won, and it can be charged to your room. Do you need anything else before I transfer your call?
Caller	No, thank you.
Operator	Now, let me transfer you to the Reservation Department.[3] Have a wonderful day, sir!

Key & Alternative Expressions

1. How may I assist you?
   = Can (May) I help you?
   = How can I help you?
   = What can I do for you?

2. Why don't you use our limousine service?
   = I recommend that you use our limousine service.
   = How about using our limousine service?
   = May I suggest using our limousine service?

3. Let me transfer you to the Reservation Department.
   = I will transfer you to the Reservation Department.
   = Let me put you through to the Reservation Department.
   = I will connect you to the Reservation Department.

B. Giving information about hotel facilities

01-02

Operator	Thank you for calling the Lunar Hotel. This is David speaking. How may I help you?
Caller	Hello. Does your hotel have a swimming pool?
Operator	We sure do, ma'am. It is located on the 5th floor inside the fitness club.
Caller	Excellent. How late is the swimming pool open?
Operator	It is open from 7 A.M. until 10 P.M.
Caller	Great! Thank you for the information.
Operator	My pleasure.

❖ Say the following sentences in English.
1 Lunar 호텔에 전화해주셔서 감사합니다.
2 호텔에 수영장이 있나요?
3 수영장은 5층 피트니스 클럽 안에 있습니다.
4 수영장은 오전 7시부터 오후 10시까지 엽니다.

C. Giving information about hotel services I

01-03

Operator	Good afternoon, Mr. Stewart. This is Gloria speaking. How may I help you?
Guest	I'd like to watch a movie in my room. How much is it?
Operator	It's 15,000 won to watch one movie and 20,000 won to watch movies all day.
Guest	Okay.
Operator	Is there anything else I can help you with?
Guest	No, thank you.

❖ Say the following sentences in English.
1 무엇을 도와드릴까요?
2 영화 한 편을 시청하는 것은 15,000원이며 종일 시청하는 것은 20,000원입니다.
3 더 도와드릴 것 있습니까?

D. Giving information about hotel services II

01-04

Operator Good evening, Ms. Smith. May I help you?
Guest Good evening. Where can I have breakfast tomorrow?
Operator You can have breakfast at the café in the lobby, or you can order room service.
Guest Thank you.
Operator Can I help you with anything else today?
Guest Yes, when is breakfast served?
Operator The breakfast buffet is served from 5 A.M. to 10 A.M., and room service is available 24 hours a day.
Guest That's good to know. I appreciate your help.
Operator You're welcome, Ms. Smith.

❖ Say the following sentences in English.
1 로비에 있는 카페에서 조식을 드실 수 있습니다.
2 조식 뷔페는 오전 5시부터 오전 10시까지 제공됩니다.
3 룸서비스는 하루 24시간 이용하실 수 있습니다.

Essential Expressions | Giving Information

1. Answering phone calls
Thank you for calling the OOO Hotel. This is OOO speaking. How may I assist you?

2. Connecting phone calls
Let me put you through
Let me transfer you   } + to (department).
Let me connect you

3. Suggesting additional help (before ending the phone call)
Do you need anything else?
Do you need any other assistance?
Is there anything else I can help you with?
Can I help you with anything else today?

Conversation II — Handling Guest Requests

A. Connecting a call to a guest's room
01-05

Operator	Good afternoon. Nova Hotel. This is Susana speaking. How may I assist you?
Caller	Hello. Would you put me through to Mr. Gilbert in room 1004?[1]
Operator	Of course, sir. Please stay on the line.[2] I will connect you.
	(A few seconds later…)
Operator	I'm sorry, but nobody is answering the phone. Can I take a message?[3]
Caller	Yes, please. Can you tell him that Harry Schultz phoned?
Operator	Certainly, sir. Could you spell your last name, please?[4]
Caller	Yes. That's S-C-H-U-L-T-Z. He's got my number.
Operator	That's S for Sam, C for Charlie, H for hotel, U for uniform, L for Love, T for Tom, and Z for Zebra?
Caller	You've got it!
Operator	Thank you, Mr. Shultz. I'll make sure Mr. Gilbert gets your message.
Caller	Thank you very much.
Operator	It was my pleasure.

Key & Alternative Expressions

1. Would you put me through to Mr. Gilbert in room 1004?
  = Can you connect (transfer) me to Mr. Gilbert's room?
  = Can I speak to Mr. Gilbert?

2. Please stay on the line.
  = Hold the line, please. = Hold on (a moment), please. = Could you please hold?
  = Would you like to hold? = Would you hold the line? = May I put you on hold?

3. Can I take a message?
  = Can I give him a message?
  = Would you like me to take a message?
  = Would you like to leave a message?
  = Do you want to leave a message?
  cf. What's your number, please?
     Does he have your number?

4. Could you spell your last name, please?
  = How do you spell your last name?
  = How is your last name spelled?

B. Connecting a guest's call to an employee in a hotel department

Agent: Sales & Marketing Agent

Operator	Good morning. Jack speaking. How can I assist you?
Caller	I'd like to speak to Mr. Lee in Sales & Marketing.
Operator	May I ask who is calling, please?
Caller	Yes, my name is Sarah White.
Operator	Certainly, Ms. White. One moment, please.
	(A few seconds later...)
Operator	I'm sorry, but the line is busy. Would you like to leave a message?
Caller	Can you try one more time?
Operator	Sure, ma'am. Let me try once again.
	(A few seconds later...)
Agent	Good morning. Michael speaking. How may I assist you?
Caller	May I speak to Mr. Lee, please?
Agent	I'm afraid Mr. Lee just stepped out of the office.
Caller	When do you expect him back?
Agent	I'm not sure, but he will probably be back by three. Shall I have him call you when he returns to the office?
Caller	No, that's all right. I'll call back later. Thank you.
Agent	My pleasure.

❖ Say the following sentences in English.
1. 누구신지 여쭤봐도 될까요?
2. 죄송하지만, 지금 통화 중이십니다.
3. 말씀 전해드릴까요?
4. 죄송하지만 Lee 씨는 방금 사무실에서 나가셨습니다.
5. 아마 3시까지는 돌아오실 겁니다.
6. 사무실에 돌아오시면 전화 드리라고 할까요?

C. Wakeup call service

Operator	Good evening. Tiffany speaking. What can I do for you?
Guest	Hello. Could you give me a wakeup call at six tomorrow morning?
Operator	Absolutely, Mr. Brown. We'll call you at 6 A.M. tomorrow. Good night, sir.
Guest	Thank you. Good night.
	(The next morning…)
Guest	Hello?
Operator	Good morning, Mr. Brown. This is your 6 A.M. wakeup call.
Guest	Thank you.
Operator	You're welcome, sir. Have a great day.

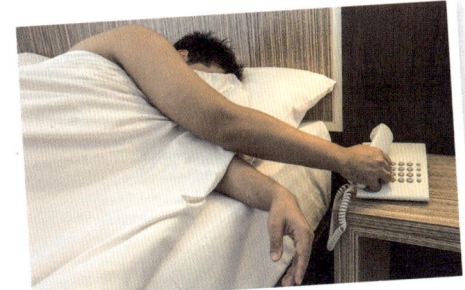

❖ Say the following sentences in English.
1 감사합니다. Tiffany입니다. 무엇을 도와드릴까요?
2 내일 아침 6시에 모닝콜 좀 해주시겠습니까?
3 좋은 아침입니다, Brown 씨. 오전 6시 모닝콜입니다.
4 좋은 하루 보내십시오.

D. Handling a wrong number

Operator	Good afternoon. Sunshine Hotel. This is Carl speaking. How may I assist you?
Caller	May I speak to Mr. James Chung in room 1105?
Operator	Just a moment, ma'am… I'm sorry, but Mr. Chung is not a guest at this hotel.
Caller	Oh, really? But he told me to call here.
Operator	I'm sorry, but there is no one here by that name. What number are you calling?
Caller	Isn't this the Sunset Hotel?
Operator	Oh, no, this is the Sunshine Hotel. I'm afraid you called the wrong hotel.

❖ Say the following sentences in English.
1 Chung 씨는 이 호텔 고객이 아닙니다.
2 죄송하지만, 여기 그런 성함을 가진 고객은 없습니다.
3 몇 번으로 전화하셨습니까?
4 죄송하지만 다른 호텔에 거셨습니다.

Essential Expressions | **Handling Guest Requests**

1. Asking for the caller's name
May I ask who is calling, please?
Who's calling, please?
Where are you calling from?
cf. I didn't catch your name.

2. When failing to connect a call
I'm sorry, but the line is busy (engaged).
I'm sorry, but nobody is answering the phone.
I'm afraid he's on another line.

Would you like to leave a message?
Would you please hold the line?
Could you call back later?

3. Promising to deliver messages (messenger service)
I'll make sure he gets your message.
I'll have him call you back.
I'll ask him to call you as soon as possible.
I'll give him the message when he comes back.
I'll tell him that you called.

4. Delivering messages
There is a message for you from Mr. White. He asked you to call him back as soon as you returned.

5. Telephone problems
I can't hear you very well.
The line is very bad.

Could you speak up a little, please?

I'm sorry. I didn't catch that (your name). Could you repeat that, please?

Exercises

A Choose the best response to each question or statement.

1. A: Would you like to leave a message?
   B: _____
   a. Yes, please.
   b. I can take a message.
   c. It would be my pleasure.

2. A: May I speak to Mr. Kim in the Sales Department?
   B: _____
   a. I'll have him call you back.
   b. He just stepped out of the office.
   c. How can I help you?

3. A: I'd like to reserve the limousine pickup service, please.
   B: _____
   a. Thank you for calling.
   b. Let me put you through to the Reservation Department.
   c. I'll make sure he gets the message.

4. A: Does your hotel have a business center?
   B: _____
   a. I'm glad to hear that.
   b. Don't mention it.
   c. Yes, we do.

B Match each sentence with the best reply.

1. Would you wake me up at 7 tomorrow morning?
2. May I ask who is calling, please?
3. Would you like to leave a message?
4. What number are you calling?
5. When do you expect him back?

a. Certainly, sir. We will call you at 7 A.M.
b. Isn't this the Ocean Hotel?
c. I think he will be back by noon.
d. No, that's all right. I'll call back later.
e. Yes, my name is Doris Bell.

C Complete the following conversation with the words in the box.

| busy | hold | connect | assist | speaking |

Operator: Good morning. This is Lisa ¹_____.
How may I ²_____ you?

Caller: Hi. Can you ³_____ me to Mr. Shaw's room?

Operator: Certainly, ma'am. I'll connect you…
I'm sorry, but the line is ⁴_____.
Would you ⁵_____ the line?

Caller: No problem.

Role-Playing

A Use the web page below to practice giving information about the hotel. Take turns being an operator and a caller with your partner.

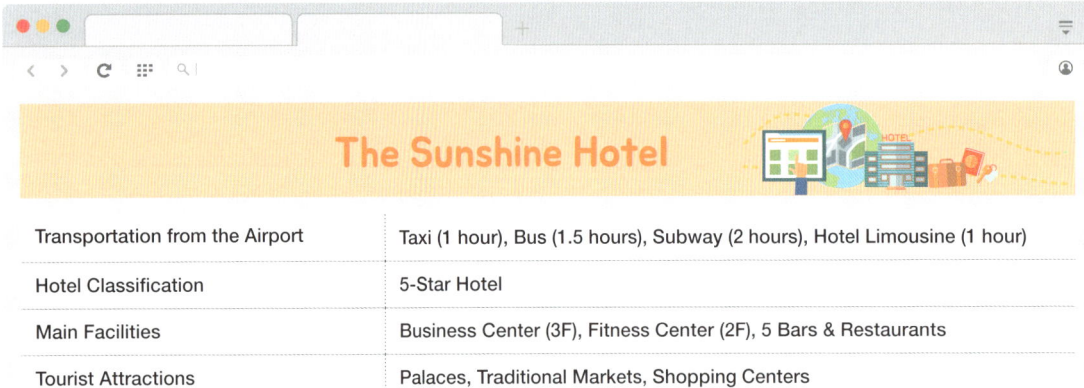

The Sunshine Hotel

Transportation from the Airport	Taxi (1 hour), Bus (1.5 hours), Subway (2 hours), Hotel Limousine (1 hour)
Hotel Classification	5-Star Hotel
Main Facilities	Business Center (3F), Fitness Center (2F), 5 Bars & Restaurants
Tourist Attractions	Palaces, Traditional Markets, Shopping Centers

Example

Operator: Good morning. Sunshine Hotel. What can I help you with?
Caller: How can I get to the hotel from the airport?
Operator: You may take a taxi, a bus, a subway, or a hotel limousine.

B Practice handling the following situations. Take turns being an operator and a caller with your partner.

Situation 1 | Connecting a call to a guest's room

Situation 2 | Connecting a guest's call to an employee in a hotel department

Situation 3 | Taking a request for a wakeup call

Situation 4 | Handling a wrong number

Example

Operator: Good morning. Castle Hotel. How may I assist you?
Caller: Can I speak to Mr. Han in room 1030?
Operator: _____.

Looking into the Hotel Read the following passage that describes what the hotel switchboard does.

01-09

Switchboard

The switchboard (PBX) at a hotel is the department which provides one of the most important services for guests. The switchboard employees are called operators, and they are ready to answer the phone around the clock. They not only connect all the phone calls at the hotel, but they also often greet hotel guests for the very first time when they call the hotel. Thus, it is important for them to make a good impression of the hotel on the guests. These operators work in the "back of the house," which is a hotel term that refers to a hidden office in a hotel that guests cannot see. They perform various tasks such as connecting phone calls, making wakeup calls, giving information and directions, and handling call charges.

Nowadays at some hotels, the switchboard functions as a one-call service or one-stop service department for the convenience of hotel guests. The operator takes orders from guests and distributes them to room service, the bell desk, housekeeping, and the front desk. Guests can therefore place all of their orders with operators at the switchboard, so there is no need to call different departments to make different orders.

Words & Phrases

around the clock for 24 hours without stopping
convenience the condition of being useful or suitable for a particular person
department a section in an organization such as a government, a business, or a university
distribute to give or deliver things to a number of people
function to serve

greet to welcome someone with polite words or actions
impression the feeling you have about someone or something, usually after having seen or heard that person or thing
perform to do a task
place an order to order

2

Reservations

Warming Up

A Look at the pictures below. What are the differences between these three types of beds? Share your thoughts with your partner.

B Which information does a reservations agent ask a guest first when taking a reservation?

a. if the guest has stayed at the hotel before

b. the number of guests

c. the room type

d. the arrival date and number of nights the guest is staying

e. the name of the guest

Vocabulary Write the correct word or phrase for each definition.

>   arrange   extra   on behalf of   available   book   guarantee

1. _____ (phrase) as the representative of someone; instead of someone
2. _____ (verb) to reserve; to arrange to have something or to use it at a particular time
3. _____ (verb) to make plans for something to happen; to make it possible for someone to do something
4. _____ (adjective) requiring additional payment; additional
5. _____ (verb) to promise that something will definitely happen
6. _____ (adjective) able to be used or bought

Hotel Terminology Learn the following words and phrases used in the hotel industry.

cancelation charge	a penalty for canceling a reservation
cancelation policy	a set of plans about what to do when guests cancel their reservations
confirmation number	a reservation number
ETA	estimated time of arrival
executive floor	a special floor in a hotel with enhanced service which is often designated for business travelers
extra bed	a rollaway bed that can be temporarily set up in a hotel room
full house	a situation in which every room is occupied
service charge	a gratuity (usually 10% of the room rate or food & beverage charge)
triple room	a room designed for three people to stay together, mostly preferred by families

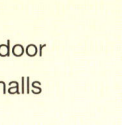
Tips to Know

Types of Hotel Rooms
- **single** a room assigned to one person (may have one bed)
- **double** a room assigned to two people (may have one or more beds)
- **triple** a room assigned to three people (may have two or more beds)
- **suite** a parlor or living room connected to one or more bedrooms
- **connecting room** a room connected to another one with a door opening between them (a connecting door)
- **adjoining rooms** rooms with a common wall but no connecting door
- **adjacent rooms** rooms close to each other, such as across the halls

Conversation 1: Taking Room Reservations

A. Taking reservations

02-01

Agent: Reservations Agent

Agent	Imperial Hotel reservations. Sandra speaking. How may I assist you?
Caller	Hi. I'd like to reserve a room, please.
Agent	What day will you be arriving, sir?[1]
Caller	On May 23.
Agent	How long will you be staying with us?[2]
Caller	I will be staying for three nights. Do you have any rooms available?[3]
Agent	Let me check… Yes, we have a deluxe room available for those days. We can offer you a deluxe room for $250 a night plus tax and service charges. Will that be suitable?
Caller	Is breakfast included?
Agent	No, breakfast is extra. You can enjoy it at the restaurant and charge the bill to your room.
Caller	That's fine. I'll take it.
Agent	May I have your name and phone number? Have you stayed with us before?
Caller	My name is Colin Sellers. This is my first visit. And my number is (202) 555-0160.
Agent	Very good, Mr. Sellers. Your room has been reserved from May 23 to 26, and your confirmation number is 17502. Thank you for calling. We look forward to seeing you then.

Key & Alternative Expressions

1. What day will you be arriving, sir?
- = When are you going to check in?
- = When do you plan to check in?
- = When would you like to stay with us?
- = What is the date of your arrival?
- = On what day will you be arriving?

2. How long will you be staying with us?
- = How many nights will you be staying?
- = How many nights do you wish to stay?

3. Do you have any rooms available?
- = Do you have any vacancies?
- = Are there any rooms available?

B. Explaining a cancelation policy

Agent: Reservations Agent

Caller	Hello? Can I speak to someone in Reservations?
Agent	This is the reservation desk. Brandon speaking. How may I help you?
Caller	I'd like to book a room for two for this Saturday night. Are there any rooms available?
Agent	Certainly, ma'am. How many nights will you be staying?
Caller	I'll just be there for one night.
Agent	Okay, ma'am. We have a double room available for this Saturday. The rate is $250 per night, including tax and service charges. Would you like to book it?
Caller	Yes, please. Oh, by the way, what is your cancelation policy?
Agent	Should you need to cancel your reservation, please let us know 24 hours prior to your scheduled arrival time.

❖ Say the following sentences in English.
1. 예약 가능한 방이 있습니까?
2. 며칠 투숙하실 예정입니까?
3. 요금은 1박에 250달러이며, 세금과 봉사료를 포함한 가격입니다.
4. (예약) 취소 규정이 어떻게 되나요?

C. Putting a customer on the waiting list

Agent: Reservations Agent

Agent	Holiday Hotel reservations. Anna speaking. How may I help you?
Caller	Hello. I'm trying to reserve a room for this weekend.
Agent	I'm awfully sorry, but we have no rooms available for this weekend. Shall I give you the number of another hotel nearby?
Caller	Well, can you just put me on the waiting list?
Agent	Of course, sir. May I have your name and contact number? If there is a cancelation, I'll let you know.

❖ Say the following sentences in English.
1. 이번 주말에 객실을 예약하고 싶은데요.
2. 정말 죄송합니다만, 이번 주말에는 예약 가능한 객실이 없습니다.
3. 근처에 있는 다른 호텔 전화번호를 안내해드릴까요?
4. 그냥 저를 대기자 명단에 넣어주실 수 있나요?

D. Taking an executive floor (EFL) room reservation

Agent: Reservations Agent

Caller	Hello. I'll be arriving on the 15th of July and will be staying until the 17th. Do you have any rooms available on the executive floor?
Agent	Yes, sir. We have rooms on the executive floor, and they include the full range of executive services.
Caller	Excellent. Can I make a reservation for that?
Agent	Certainly. May I have your name, please?
Caller	I'm Joseph Lee from New York. I'm a gold-level member of your hotel.
Agent	It's nice to have you back, Mr. Lee. Would you like to use the same credit card on file? It's a MasterCard.
Caller	No, I want to use my Visa card.
Agent	Could you give me the credit card number to guarantee the reservation?
Caller	Sure. The number is 4485 5320 8157 6223, and the expiration date is December 25, 2025.
Agent	All right, sir. You're all set. Your confirmation number is 17503. Is there anything else I can help you with?
Caller	Yes. Do you have limousine service from the airport?
Agent	We sure do. Please let me know your flight number and your time of arrival. I'll arrange it for you.

❖ Say the following sentences in English.
1 비지니스전용층에 예약 가능한 방이 있나요?
2 다시 모시게 되어 반갑습니다, Lee 씨.
3 저희 기록에 있는 신용카드를 사용하시겠습니까?
4 예약을 보장하기 위해 신용카드 번호를 말씀해주시겠습니까?
5 다 되셨습니다.
6 비행기 편명과 도착 예정 시각을 말씀해주십시오.

E. Handling special requests

Agent: Reservations Agent

Agent   Good morning. Hillside Hotel reservations. Aaron speaking. How may I assist you?

Caller   I would like to reserve a room for my family vacation. Can you recommend a room for me?

Agent   Certainly. When are you going to check in, ma'am?

Caller   On March 10 for 3 nights.

Agent   How many are you in your family?

Caller   We're a family of four. I'm traveling with my husband and 2 children.

Agent   How old are your kids?

Caller   They are 10 and 8 years old.

Agent   Well... I recommend that you book connecting rooms or a triple room with an extra bed in it. Which one do you prefer?

Caller   A triple room with an extra bed will be fine. I would like to be in the same room as my kids. What is the room rate?

Agent   It's $230 a night, and there is a $30 charge for an extra bed.

Caller   Can I have a room with an ocean view?

Agent   I'm afraid that I can't guarantee a room with that view. However, I'll make a special request to the front desk.

❖ Say the following sentences in English.
1. 가족이 몇 분이십니까?
2. 자녀분들 나이가 어떻게 되십니까?
3. 침대를 추가하셔서 30달러의 요금이 있습니다.

Essential Expressions | **Taking Room Reservations**

1. Asking a guest the number of people to stay
How many people will be staying in the room?
How many are you in your party (group/family)?
How many people is the reservation for?
How many adults will be in the room?

2. Saying that a hotel has a full house
We are fully booked for that period.
We are completely booked for Christmas this year.
We have no rooms available for this weekend.
We don't have any rooms available until the 18th of this month.
All our single rooms are reserved. The only room we have available is a twin room.

Unit 2 | 27

Conversation II: Handling Requests After Reservations

A. Confirming reservations

Agent: Reservations Agent

Agent	Good afternoon. Jade Hotel. Amy speaking. How may I assist you?
Caller	I'd like to confirm my reservation, please. Can you help me with that?
Agent	Absolutely, sir. Could you tell me your name and reservation number?
Caller	My name is Hugo Hunter, but I'm afraid I don't remember my reservation number.
Agent	That's all right. Let me check on that...[1] Mr. Hunter, you reserved a double room for 2 nights starting on August 15.[2] You requested a nonsmoking room on a high floor.
Caller	That's right. Can you send me a confirmation email?
Agent	Certainly, sir. I'll send it to you right away.
Caller	Thank you.
Agent	My pleasure, sir.[3]

Key & Alternative Expressions

1. Let me check on that.
= Let me check your reservation details.
= Let me check if we have your reservation (on the system).
= Let me look you up on the system.

2. You reserved a double room for 2 nights starting on August 15.
= You will be staying in a double room for 2 nights starting on August 15.
= We have a reservation for you from August 15 to August 17.
= You are going to stay with us for 2 nights starting on August 15. Is that correct?

3. My pleasure, sir.
= It was my pleasure, sir. = You're welcome, sir.
= I'm happy to help, sir. = No problem, sir.

B. Changing reservations

Agent: Reservations Agent

Caller　Hello. My name is Roy McDonald.
　　　　I'd like to change my reservation, please.
Agent　Certainly, Mr. McDonald.
　　　　Do you have the reservation number?
Caller　I'm afraid not.
Agent　That's all right. Let me check on that.
　　　　One moment, please…
　　　　You have a reservation for a deluxe twin room for 3 nights starting on May 23.
Caller　That's correct. But can I change the arrival date to May 11?
Agent　Just a moment… Okay, sir. I've changed that for you.
　　　　Your reservation number is 17110.
Caller　I appreciate it.
Agent　You're welcome, sir. We will see you on May 11.

❖ Say the following sentences in English.
1 예약을 변경하고 싶습니다.
2 확인해보겠습니다.
3 디럭스 트윈룸으로 5월 23일부터 3박 예약되어 있으시네요.
4 그렇게 변경해드렸습니다.

C. Canceling reservations

02-08

Agent: Reservations Agent

Caller	I'd like to cancel a reservation, please.
Agent	May I have your name and reservation number?
Caller	I'm calling on behalf of Mr. David Johns. The reservation number is 17157. It is a reservation for June 15.
Agent	Excuse me, but may I ask who is calling?
Caller	I'm Julia Green, Mr. Johns's secretary.
Agent	Sure. May I ask why he is canceling? And can I have your phone number?
Caller	No problem. His business trip to Korea has been canceled, and my number is (305) 321-6542.
Agent	Thank you. I've canceled his reservation. We hope to serve him the next time he is in town.

❖ Say the following sentences in English.
1 예약을 취소하려고 합니다.
2 David Johns 씨 대신 전화 드렸습니다.
3 실례지만, 전화 주신 분은 어떻게 되십니까?
4 그분의 예약을 취소해드렸습니다.

Essential Expressions | **Handling Requests After Reservations**

1. Expressing strong agreement
Absolutely. / Certainly.
Of course. / Very good.

2. Confirming reservations, changes, and cancelations
Your reservation has been made (changed/canceled).
I've made (changed/canceled) your reservation for you.

3. Saying goodbye to a guest who just canceled a reservation
We look forward to serving you next time.
We hope to serve you next time.
Please call again the next time you visit.
Please remember us in the future.

Exercises

A Choose the best response to each question or statement.

1. A: Do you have any rooms available?
   B: _____
   a. Yes, we have 350 rooms in total.
   b. I'd like to reserve a room.
   c. I'm afraid we have a full house today.

2. A: We're a family of three. Can you recommend a room for us?
   B: _____
   a. How about staying in a triple room?
   b. The single rooms are all booked.
   c. You can come in with your children.

3. A: What is the room rate?
   B: _____
   a. I can offer you a room for $200 a night.
   b. Tax and service charges are included.
   c. You can get a group discount.

4. A: Do you want me to give you the number of another hotel nearby?
   B: _____
   a. Can I have your name?
   b. Yes, that would be great.
   c. I'm very sorry, sir.

B Match each sentence with the best reply.

1. Is breakfast included?
2. How many nights will you be staying?
3. Have you stayed with us before?
4. What is your cancelation policy?
5. Can you put me on the waiting list?

a. I'm going to stay for two nights.
b. Please let us know 24 hours prior to your scheduled arrival time.
c. No, this is my first trip to Korea.
d. Certainly. If there is a cancelation, I'll let you know.
e. I'm afraid breakfast is extra.

C Complete the following conversation with the words in the box.

> including   staying   arriving   offer   vacancies

Agent: Good morning. White Hotel. Miranda speaking. May I help you?
Caller: Do you have any ¹_____?
Agent: What day will you be ²_____?
Caller: On May 5, and I'll be ³_____ for a week.
Agent: I can ⁴_____ you a deluxe room for $250 per night, ⁵_____ tax and service charges.
Caller: Very good. I will take it.

Role-Playing

A Use the room tariffs below to practice taking room reservations on the phone. Take turns being a reservations agent and a caller with your partner.

Sunshine Hotel Room Tariffs

○ **Standard Rooms**
Deluxe — $200
Grand Deluxe — $250

○ **Executive Rooms**
Deluxe — $300
Grand Deluxe — $350

○ **Suites**
Superior — $500
Royal — $800
Presidential — $1,000

The above rates are subject to a 10% service charge and a 10% government tax.

Example

Agent	Thank you for calling. Sunshine Hotel reservations. Jane speaking. How may I assist you?
Caller	Do you have any rooms available?
Agent	What type of room would you like?
Caller	_____.

B Use the confirmation mail below to practice confirming and canceling reservations. Take turns being a reservations agent and a caller with your partner.

◊ Reservation Confirmation ◊

Dear Mr. Smith,

Thank you for choosing to stay with us at the Mirage Hotel. We are pleased to confirm your reservation as follows:

Confirmation Number:	237029
Guest Name:	Mr. Smith, John
Arrival Date:	05/15/2021
Departure Date:	05/18/2021
Number of Guests:	2
Accommodations:	Royal Suite
Rate per Night:	$800.00
Check-in Time	3:00 P.M.
Checkout Time	12:00 P.M.

Rates are subject to applicable state and local taxes. If you need to cancel this reservation, the Mirage Hotel requires notification by 3:00 P.M. the day before your arrival to avoid a charge for one night's room rate.

Should you have any requests, please feel free to call us at 1-800-800-8000 or email us at reservations@mirage.com.

We look forward to the pleasure of having you as our guest at the Mirage Hotel.

Sincerely,

Sandra Jones
Reservations Department

Example

Agent	Thank you for calling. Reservations. Sandra speaking. How may I assist you?
Caller	I'd like to confirm/cancel my reservation, please.
Agent	_____.

Looking into the Hotel Read the following passage that describes what the Reservation Department does.

02-09

Reservations

Reservations can be made in various ways, such as by telephone, travel agent, fax, letter, the Internet, and email, and there are also walk-in guests. Nowadays, one can easily book a hotel room online without having to speak a word. However, there are still many people who prefer talking to a person when they reserve a room. These potential guests call hotels and talk to the agents in the Reservation Department. Reservations agents mainly work in hidden offices like operators do. Guests call them to make inquiries, and then they decide whether to stay or not. That is why the reservation agents must have excellent communication skills and phone etiquette when speaking with guests.

When receiving a phone call, the reservations agent should first ask when the guest will arrive at the hotel and how long he or she will stay there. If there are any available rooms, the agent will ask about the type of room the guest wants. The agent will also ask the guest's name and his or her credit card number to guarantee the reservation and then find out if there are any other special requests.

During the peak season, reservations agents sometimes overbook rooms in case there are any cancelations or no-shows. By doing that, the hotel tries to have a full house to maximize its profits. However, overbooking can sometimes mean the hotel has to turn away some of its guests and send them to other hotels. Therefore, overbooking should be done carefully.

Words & Phrases

etiquette rules indicating the proper and polite way to behave
guarantee to promise that something will definitely happen
have a full house to have no vacancy; to be fully booked
inquiry a question which you ask in order to get some information

no-show a person who is expected to be somewhere but does not show up
overbook to accept reservations in excess of the available space
turn away to send someone to another hotel due to overbooking
walk-in guest a guest who arrives with no reservation

3
Door & Bell Desk

Warming Up

A Look at the two pictures below. Who are they? What do they do? Share your thoughts with your partner.

B Choose the picture that shows something a bellman does NOT do.

a. 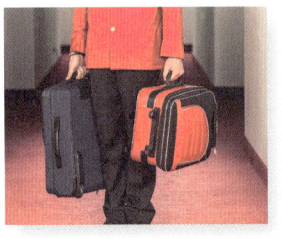   b.    c.    d.

Vocabulary
Write the correct word or phrase for each definition.

| inconvenience | revolving door | shelf |
| escort | spacious | unload |

1. _____ (noun) a set of doors that you go through by pushing them around in a circle
2. _____ (noun) something causing problems or difficulties
3. _____ (verb) to take goods from a car
4. _____ (verb) to take someone somewhere
5. _____ (adjective) large in size or area; roomy; huge; large
6. _____ (noun) a flat piece of wood, glass, or metal used to keep things on

Hotel Terminology
Learn the following words and phrases used in the hotel industry.

baggage claim tag	a ticket given to hotel guests to prove that the baggage is theirs
baggage down service	a service that brings guests' baggage down to the lobby; a baggage collection service
bellman	a man who carries guests' bags in a hotel; a bellhop; a bellboy
checkroom	a room in a hotel where guests can leave their coats and other personal things; a cloakroom
doorman	a man who stands by the door of a hotel and lets people in or out
minibar	a small fridge in a hotel room, with beverages and light snacks inside
paging service	a service in which a bellman calls the names of guests to find them for other guests in a public place or to take messages from guests to other guests
safe	a strong metal box with a lock where people can keep their money or valuable things in a guest room
valet parking	a service in which guests' cars are parked for them

Tips to Know

Doorman vs. Bellman

What's the difference between a doorman and a bellman? The major difference is the working area on the hotel premises. A doorman works in the area outside the hotel lobby and handles all the guest services that take place outdoors. On the other hand, a bellman works in the hotel lobby and visits almost all of the indoor places on the hotel premises, including the guest rooms.

Conversation 1: Doorman Service

A. Welcoming a guest

Doorman Good morning, ma'am. Welcome to the Golden Hotel. Do you have any bags that I can help you with?
Guest Yes. I have a couple of bags in the trunk.
Doorman Let me unload them, ma'am. Our bellman will take care of your baggage afterward.
Guest That's nice. Where do I register?[1]
Doorman The front desk is over there to your left. Please watch out for the revolving door.
Guest Thank you.
Doorman It's my pleasure. Have a good stay with us.[2]

B. Helping a guest with a taxi

Doorman Good afternoon, ma'am. Would you like a taxi?[3]
Guest Yes, please. I'm going to Namdaemun Market.
Doorman Please have a seat in the lobby, ma'am. I'll let you know when one is ready for you.
Guest Thank you. How long does it take to get there from here?
Doorman Well, it normally takes about 10 minutes,[4] but it may take longer depending on traffic.

Key & Alternative Expressions

1. **Where do I register?**
   = Where is the front desk? = Where can I check in? = Where is the reception desk?

2. **Have a good stay with us.**
   = Please enjoy your stay (with us). = Have a nice stay (with us). = I wish you a wonderful stay with us.

3. **Would you like a taxi?**
   = Do you need a taxi (cab)? = Shall I call a taxi (cab) for you? = Do you want me to catch (grab) a taxi (cab) for you?

4. **It normally takes about 10 minutes.**
   = It takes 10 minutes on foot (by taxi / by subway / by bus) from here.
   = It is 10 minutes away from here.
   = It is a 10-minute walk (drive) from here.

C. Valet parking services I

03-03

Doorman   Good afternoon, ma'am. Can I help you?
Guest   Where should I park my car?
Doorman   You can use our valet parking service.
          Just leave your car here.
          I will have someone take care of everything.
Guest   Great. Thank you.
Doorman   You're welcome, ma'am.

❖ Say the following sentences in English.
1 차를 어디에다 대야 하나요?
2 그냥 여기에 차를 두고 가십시오.
3 담당 직원에게 처리하라고 하겠습니다.

D. Valet parking services II

03-04

Doorman   Good evening, ma'am. What can I do for you?
Guest   Could you get my car, please?
Doorman   Of course, ma'am. What's the plate number?
Guest   The number is 4577. It's a black car.
Doorman   I'll bring it immediately.
          Just one moment, please.
Guest   Thank you very much.
Doorman   My pleasure.

❖ Say the following sentences in English.
1 제 차를 가져다주시겠습니까?
2 차량 번호가 어떻게 되십니까?
3 고객님의 차를 즉시 가져오겠습니다.

E. Saying farewell to a guest

03-05

Doorman   Good morning, ma'am. Are you leaving now?
Guest   Yes, I am.
Doorman   Did you enjoy your stay with us?
Guest   Yes, I had a wonderful time.
I'll definitely come back here again!
Doorman   I'm pleased to hear that.
Do you need a taxi?
Guest   Yes, I do.
(Doorman waves to a taxi standing by...)
Doorman   Here comes a taxi.
I'll put your luggage in the trunk.
Guest   Thank you so much.
Doorman   Enjoy your trip, ma'am.

❖ **Say the following sentences in English.**
1 지금 가십니까?
2 저희 호텔에서 편안하게 쉬셨습니까?
3 그 말씀을 들으니 기쁩니다.
4 택시가 필요하십니까?
5 택시가 오네요.
6 제가 짐을 트렁크에 실어드리겠습니다.

Essential Expressions | Doorman Service

1. Greeting a guest in front of the door
Good morning (afternoon/evening), ma'am (sir).
Welcome to the Golden Hotel.

Do you have any bags that I can help you with?
Do you have any luggage with you?
May I help you with your luggage?

2. Saying that a bellman will take care of a guest's baggage
Our bellman will take care of your baggage.
A bellman will take your bags to your room.
Our bellboy will assist you with your luggage.

3. Asking a guest to be careful
Please watch out for the revolving door.
Watch your step. The road is slippery.
Mind your head, please.

4. Suggesting a guest to wait inside
Please have a seat in the lobby. I'll let you know when a taxi is ready.
Would you like to wait inside, ma'am? I will call you when a cab arrives.

Conversation II: Bellman Service

A. Taking a guest to his or her room
03-06

Bellman	Good afternoon, ma'am. Are these all your bags, ma'am?[1]
Guest	Yes, these are all of them.
Bellman	May I have your keycard?
Guest	Here it is.
Bellman	Thank you. Let me escort you to your room, ma'am. This way, please…[2] Please take the elevator. After you, ma'am.[3]
Guest	Thanks.
Bellman	Your room is on the 16th floor… Here we are. After you, ma'am.
	(They get out of the elevator.)
Bellman	Your room is on the right side. This way, please.
	(They arrive at the door.)
Bellman	This is your room. Please go in. Where shall I put your bags?
Guest	Over there is fine. Thanks. This room is nicer and more spacious than I expected. I love the view overlooking downtown.
Bellman	I'm glad you like the room, ma'am.

Key & Alternative Expressions

1. **Are these all your bags, ma'am?**
   = Is there any other baggage?
   = Do you have any other bags?
   = How many pieces of baggage do you have?

2. **This way, please.**
   = Please come with me.
   = Please follow me.
   = Step this way, please.

3. **After you, ma'am.**
   = Please go first.

Unit 3 | 39

B. Showing a guest his or her room

03-07

Bell Captain Let me show you your room, sir.
Here is the light switch for the bathroom.
The temperature controller is right here.
A safe is in the built-in closet right there.
Your minibar is in the cabinet over there, and the price list is on the shelf. You'll get charged for what you use when you check out. There are two bottles of complimentary mineral water on the shelf.

Guest You've been very helpful. This is for you.

Bell Captain I'm sorry, sir. Our hotel has a no-tipping policy. A service charge will be added to your final bill.

Guest Oh, really? Thank you.

Bell Captain The pleasure is all mine, sir. Enjoy your stay. If you need any other assistance, please call the bell desk at any time.

❖ Say the following sentences in English.
1 제가 객실을 보여드리겠습니다.
2 사용하신 것은 체크아웃하실 때 청구될 겁니다.
3 무료 생수 두 병이 선반 위에 있습니다.
4 저희 호텔은 팁을 받지 않습니다.
5 봉사료는 최종 계산서에 합산될 겁니다.

C. Baggage down service

Bell Captain	Good morning. This is the bell desk. Peter speaking. How may I assist you?
Guest	Good morning. Can you send a bellman to my room? I'm checking out in 10 minutes.
Bell Captain	No problem, ma'am. May I have your name and room number?
Guest	I'm Clara Hansen in room 1021.
Bell Captain	Thank you, Ms. Hansen. How many bags do you have?
Guest	I have two suitcases and one carry-on bag.
Bell Captain	I see. I will send someone up immediately.

❖ Say the following sentences in English.
1. 제 방으로 벨맨을 보내주시겠습니까?
2. 저는 10분 후에 체크아웃할 예정입니다.
3. 가방이 몇 개나 되십니까?
4. 여행용 가방 2개와 휴대용 가방 1개가 있습니다.
5. 지금 바로 직원을 올려보내겠습니다.

D. Holding baggage

Bellman	Good morning, ma'am. How may I help you?
Guest	Hi. Can my husband and I leave our bags at the hotel? We just checked out of our room, but we would like to go downtown to look around before leaving for the airport.
Bellman	Sure. Let me store your luggage in our checkroom until you come back. Can I have your name and room number?
Guest	I'm Shirley Carson, and I was in room 1004.
Bellman	I see, Mrs. Carson. Are these your only bags?
Guest	Yes. These three suitcases.
Bellman	All right. Here is your baggage claim tag. Please keep this until you pick up your bags. Have a great time.

❖ Say the following sentences in English.
1. 저와 남편 가방을 호텔에 두고 가도 되나요?
2. 돌아오실 때까지 짐을 보관소에 보관해드리겠습니다.
3. 성함과 객실 번호를 알 수 있을까요?
4. 이 가방들이 전부입니까?
5. 수하물보관증 여기 있습니다.

E. Handling complaints about baggage delivery

03-10

Bell Captain Good afternoon. This is the bell desk. Alan speaking. Can I help you?

Guest Yes, I'm Rose Baker in room 528. I've been waiting for my bags to be sent up for almost 30 minutes!

Bell Captain I'm terribly sorry for the delay, Ms. Baker. Do you have a baggage tag number?

Guest Yes. It's 0132.

Bell Captain I'll check on that right away and get back to you, ma'am.

(A few minutes later...)

Bell Captain Hello. This is the bell captain. Alan speaking. Ms. Baker, your bags are on the way now. I'm very sorry for the inconvenience.

❖ **Say the following sentences in English.**
1. 거의 30분째 가방이 올라오기를 기다리고 있다고요!
2. 지연이 되어 대단히 죄송합니다, Baker 씨.
3. 제가 바로 확인해보고 다시 전화 드리겠습니다.
4. 고객님 가방이 지금 올라가는 중입니다.
5. 불편을 끼쳐드려 정말 죄송합니다.

Essential Expressions | Bellman Service

1. Asking guests where to put their bags
   Where shall I put your bags?
   Shall I put your bags over there?
   I will put your bags over here.

2. Promising further assistance
   If you need any other assistance, please call the bell desk at any time.
   If you need anything, please feel free to contact us.
   If you need any help, please dial 0.

3. Checking in baggage
   Let me store your luggage in our checkroom until you come back.
   We can keep your bags for you.
   You can check your luggage at the bell desk.
   We will hold your baggage until you come for it.

4. Apologizing politely
   I'm very (terribly/extremely/awfully) sorry for the inconvenience.
   I apologize for the inconvenience.
   Please accept our sincere apology.

Exercises

A Choose the best response to each question.

1. Who works outside the hotel premises?
   a. a bell captain
   b. a cashier
   c. a doorman

2. Where can guests store their bags after they check out?
   a. at the front desk
   b. in the checkroom
   c. in their rooms

3. Which is one of the responsibilities of the bellman?
   a. valet parking
   b. showing guests their rooms
   c. delivering food

4. Who is the first employee a guest will meet after arriving at a hotel?
   a. a bellman
   b. a receptionist
   c. a doorman

B Match each sentence with the best reply.

1. Where do I register?
2. Can you call a taxi for me?
3. Could you get my car?
4. Where shall I put your bags, ma'am?
5. I've been waiting for my bags for about 30 minutes!

a. I'm very sorry for the inconvenience.
b. The front desk is right over there.
c. No problem, sir. What's the plate number?
d. Over there, please.
e. Absolutely. Please have a seat in the lobby while you wait.

C Complete the following conversation with the words in the box.

> get   after   complimentary   charged   way

Bellman: Let me escort you to your room, ma'am. This ¹_____, please… Please take the elevator. ²_____ you, ma'am… This is your room. Please ³_____ in. Where shall I put your bags?

Guest: Over there is fine. Thanks.

Bellman: There is a minibar in the cabinet.

Guest: Are the items in it ⁴_____?

Bellman: I'm afraid not. You'll get ⁵_____ for what you use when you check out. Only the two bottles of mineral water outside the minibar are free daily.

Role-Playing

A Practice welcoming and helping a guest. Take turns being a doorman and a guest with your partner.

Example

Doorman: Good morning, ma'am. Welcome to the Cosmos Hotel.
Guest: Can you help with my baggage in the trunk?
Doorman: _____.

B Practice escorting a guest to his room and helping him with his baggage. Take turns being a bellman and a guest.

Example

Bellman: Good afternoon, sir. May I have your room key?
Guest: Here it is.
Bellman: _____.

Looking into the Hotel — Read the following passage that describes what the workers at the door and bell desk do.

Door and Bell Desks

The door desk is located outside the hotel's main entrance. It is the department whose workers greet guests first and see them off last. When a guest's car arrives, a doorman opens the car door and says hello to the guest with a warm smile. Doormen are in charge of the parking area, so they provide valet parking service themselves, and they sometimes call taxis for hotel guests.

The bell desk is located in the lobby near the concierge desk or main entrance. When a guest arrives, a bellman helps the guests with his or her baggage and carries it to the front desk. Then, he waits until the guest finishes the check-in process.

Once the guest gets a room key, the bellman takes the guest to his or her room and explains what is in the room. When the guest checks out, the bellman takes the guest's baggage down to the lobby. This is not the only job bellmen do though. They deliver messages, mail, and packages to guests in their rooms and page guests as well. When guests don't answer wakeup calls, bellmen sometimes wake up the guests in person by knocking on their doors or even going into their rooms. A full-service hotel can have the bell desk open for 24 hours like the front desk.

As doormen and bellmen often give the first and last impressions of the hotel for guests, good language skills along with a helpful and friendly attitude are required for these positions.

Words & Phrases

concierge an employee who helps guests with information about the area where the hotel is, including transportation, restaurants, and tours
main entrance the main door
package a box that is sent by mail
see off to take someone to a point of departure to say goodbye

4

Front Desk I (Reception)

Warming Up

A Look at the picture below. Where in a hotel is this place? What kinds of activities can take place here? Share your thoughts with your partner.

B Which item is NOT necessary for check-in?

a.  b.  c.  d.

Unit Objectives
◇ Check-In Service
◇ In-House Guest Service

Vocabulary Write the correct word or phrase for each definition.

| extend | imprint | set | inventory |
| closet | lock out | fill out | get through |

1. _____ (phrase) to write all the necessary information on a document
2. _____ (phrase) to prevent someone from entering by locking a door
3. _____ (noun) a mark left by an object when it is printed or pressed onto something
4. _____ (verb) to make something last longer
5. _____ (phrase) to reach; to succeed in making contact
6. _____ (adjective) ready; prepared
7. _____ (noun) a list of all the things that are available
8. _____ (noun) a small room with a door used to keep things in; a wardrobe

Hotel Terminology Learn the following words and phrases used in the hotel industry.

adjoining room	a room next to another with a common wall between them but without a connecting door
courtesy shuttle bus	a free shuttle bus for a hotel's guests
OTA	online travel agency
PMS	property management system
receptionist	an employee who helps guests who call or enter a hotel
registration	the process of checking guests into a hotel by recording necessary information about them in a hotel system
room assignment	the process of giving a guest a certain room
shift	a particular period of work time during the day or night
walk-in guest	a guest with no reservation; a walk-in

Tips to Know

How to Calculate a Hotel Room Rate

Most of the hotels in Korea have a no-tipping policy. Instead, a service charge is included in the room rate. The rate is subject to a 10% service charge, and a 10% government tax is applied to the sum again. This means that you have to pay an extra 21% on your room rate. Let's put it this way. If the room rate is $100 per night, the service charge will be $10, and that will bring the total to $110. Thus, the government tax will be $11. So the total amount of money you have to pay for one night is $121 ($110 + $11).

Unit 4 | 47

Conversation 1: Check-In Service

A. Check-in process I

Receptionist	Welcome to the Imperial. How may I help you?
Guest	Hi. I would like to check in, please.[1]
Receptionist	Do you have a reservation?[2]
Guest	Yes, I made a reservation on your website.
Receptionist	Under what name is your reservation, sir?[3]
Guest	It's under my name, Eric Pitt.
Receptionist	Let me check your reservation… Ah, here it is. You booked a deluxe room for two nights, so you are checking out on Saturday, right?
Guest	That's correct.
Receptionist	Did you request a nonsmoking room facing the ocean?
Guest	Yes, I did. Do you have one of those rooms on a high floor?
Receptionist	Let me see… Yes, we have a room available on the 10th floor. It is a nonsmoking room with an ocean view.
Guest	That sounds perfect.

Key & Alternative Expressions

1. **I would like to check in, please.**
   = Can I check in?
   = I have a reservation.

2. **Do you have a reservation?**
   = Did you make a reservation?
   = Have you made a reservation?
   = Did you reserve a hotel room?

3. **Under what name is your reservation, sir?**
   = May I have the name the reservation is under?
   = What is the name?

B. Check-in process II   04-02

Receptionist	May I have your business card for registration, Mr. Pitt?
Guest	Oh, I don't have one with me now.
Receptionist	Then could you fill out this registration form?
Guest	Sure.
Receptionist	While you are filling out the registration form, may I have your credit card to make an imprint?
Guest	Here you go.
Receptionist	Thank you, Mr. Pitt. You're all set. Here is your room key. You can take the elevator on your right.
Guest	Thank you very much.
Receptionist	The bellman will take you up to your room. He will take care of your baggage as well. Checkout time is at noon. If you have any questions, press 0 on the room phone.
Guest	Wonderful!
Receptionist	Thank you, and enjoy your stay with us, sir.

❖ Say the following sentences in English.
1 등록을 위해 명함을 받을 수 있을까요?
2 이 등록카드를 작성해주시겠습니까?
3 각인을 위해 신용카드를 받을 수 있을까요?
4 벨맨이 객실까지 모셔다드릴 것입니다.
5 문의 사항이 있으시면, 객실 전화로 0번을 눌러주십시오.

C. Checking in walk-in guests   04-03

Receptionist	Good evening, ma'am. Can I help you with anything?
Guest	Yes. I don't have a reservation. But do you have a room available for two nights?
Receptionist	I will check for you… We only have a deluxe room available for two nights. We can offer you that room at a rate of $280 a night plus tax and service charge.
Guest	Is that the best rate you can offer?
Receptionist	Yes, that's the best I can do for you, ma'am.
Guest	It looks like I have no choice. I guess I'll take it.
Receptionist	All right. May I have your picture ID and a credit card to secure the reservation, please?

❖ Say the following sentences in English.
1 이틀간 숙박 가능한 방 있습니까?
2 그 객실을 1박당 280달러에 세금 및 봉사료 별도로 제공해드릴 수 있습니다.

D. Checking in guests with reservation problems

(Guest walks into the lobby late at night…)

Guest Hello. Can I check in?
My name is David Ridgeway, and I made a reservation through an online travel agency.

Receptionist Just one moment, please.
Let me check your reservation.
How do you spell your last name?

Guest R-I-D-G-E-W-A-Y.

Receptionist Hmm… I'm very sorry, but we don't have a reservation under that name.
Do you have a confirmation number?

Guest I'm afraid not.

Receptionist When did you make a reservation?

Guest About 2 hours ago.

Receptionist I see. Your reservation probably hasn't gotten through to our system yet.
I will check you in now, and I will confirm your reservation as soon as the Reservation Department opens tomorrow. How long will you be staying?

Guest Three nights.

Receptionist Can I have your credit card to make an imprint, please?

Guest Sure, here it is.

❖ Say the following sentences in English.
1. 정말 죄송하지만, 고객님 성함으로 예약된 내역이 없습니다.
2. 예약번호를 가지고 계십니까?
3. 지금 체크인해드리고, 내일 예약부가 여는 대로 고객님의 예약을 확정해드리겠습니다.

Essential Expressions — Check-In Service

1. Telling a guest a room rate
We can offer you a room at a rate of $200 a night plus (excluding) tax and service charge.
The rate is $200 per night, including tax and service charge.
It is $200 a night, and a 10% tax and service charge will be added to the rate.

2. Asking for a credit card to make an imprint
May I have your credit card to make an imprint?
Can I have your credit card to make an imprint of it?
May I have your credit card to imprint it?

3. Asking about a preferred type of room
What kind (type) of room would you like?
Would you prefer a nonsmoking or smoking room?
Do you have any preference for the room?

Conversation II: In-House Guest Service

A. Changing rooms

Agent: Front Desk Agent

Agent Front Desk. Ethan speaking. How may I help you, Ms. Gilmore?

Guest Hi. Is it possible to change my room?[1] I want to move closer to my friend's room. She is staying in room 605, and her name is Ashley Anderson. Do you have something like an adjoining room next to hers?[2]

Agent Let me check.... We have a room on the 6th floor, but it is not right next to her room. It is on the opposite side of the hall. Is that okay with you, Ms. Gilmore?

Guest That's fine. I will take it.

Agent All right, ma'am. When would you like to change rooms?

Guest Anytime is fine. I'm leaving in about half an hour and not coming back until late at night. I'd appreciate it if you would move my luggage while I'm out.[3]

Agent Certainly, ma'am. In that case, could you pack your belongings before you leave? I will send a bellman up to your room and have him move your stuff to the new room. But you don't need to pack the clothes hanging in the closet.

Guest Excellent! Thank you so much.

Agent Anytime, Ms. Gilmore.

Key & Alternative Expressions

1. **Is it possible to change my room?**
   = Can I change my room?
   = I'd like to change my room.

2. **Do you have something like an adjoining room next to hers?**
   cf. Do you have two rooms close to each other?
   Do you have connecting rooms?
   Do you have a room on the same floor?

3. **I'd appreciate it if you would move my luggage while I'm out.**
   = Will it be done until I'm back (till I return / till I come back)?
   = Will it be done when (until / before / by the time) I get back?

B. Guest inquiries about a hotel shuttle service

04-06

Agent: Front Desk Agent

Agent Front desk. Nicole speaking. Can I do anything for you, Mr. Simmons?
Guest Hi. Do you provide a shuttle service for hotel guests to the downtown area?
Agent Yes, we do, sir. We operate a courtesy shuttle bus between the hotel and downtown every hour. You can get detailed information at the concierge's desk.
Guest That sounds good. What time is the last shuttle bus from here?
Agent The last shuttle bus leaves the hotel at 9 P.M.
Guest Oh, I see. Thank you for your assistance.
Agent I'm happy to help, sir.

❖ Say the following sentences in English.
1 호텔 투숙객에게 시내로 가는 셔틀 서비스를 제공합니까?
2 매시간 호텔과 시내를 오가는 무료 셔틀버스를 운행합니다.
3 마지막 셔틀버스는 오후 9시에 호텔에서 출발합니다.

C. Assisting a locked-out guest

04-07

Agent: Front Desk Agent

Agent Good evening, sir. May I help you?
Guest Good evening. I'm locked out of my room. I think I left the key in my room this morning.
Agent May I have your name and room number?
Guest My name is Henry Kwon. I'm in room 1030. Can you just make another key, please? I need one more for my wife as well.
Agent Certainly, Mr. Kwon. Could I see some picture ID, please?
Guest Here you go.
Agent Thank you, sir. Here are your room keys.

❖ Say the following sentences in English.
1 문이 잠겨서 방에 못 들어가고 있습니다.
2 사진이 나온 신분증을 보여주시겠습니까?

D. Guest inquiries about hotel facilities

Agent: Front Desk Agent

Agent   Good morning, Ms. Wilson. How can I help you?
Guest   Hello. Is there a swimming pool in this hotel?
Agent   Yes, it is. It is in the fitness club on the 3rd floor. You can also find a gym, a sauna, a barbershop, and a beauty salon in it.
Guest   Can I use the pool for free?
Agent   Yes, Ms. Wilson. The pool and the gym are complimentary for all of our hotel guests.
Guest   Great. I'll definitely stop by to work out after breakfast. Where can I have breakfast?
Agent   You can have it at the café on the 1st floor. It serves breakfast from 5:30 A.M. to 10:00 A.M.
Guest   I'm in room 1212. Is breakfast included in the price?
Agent   Let me check on that, ma'am… Yes, your package includes a daily breakfast for two.

❖ Say the following sentences in English.
1 수영장과 체육관은 모든 호텔 투숙객에게 무료입니다.
2 조식은 언제 먹을 수 있습니까?
3 카페는 오전 5시 30분부터 오전 10시까지 조식을 제공합니다.
4 조식이 가격에 포함되어 있습니까?
5 고객님의 패키지에는 일일 조식 2인분이 포함되어 있습니다.

E. Extending a stay & providing an extra bed

04-09

Agent: Front Desk Agent

- **Agent** Good afternoon, sir. How may I help you?
- **Guest** Hi. Can I extend my stay for another night?
- **Agent** Absolutely. Let me check if the room is available. May I have your room number?
- **Guest** Yes, I'm in room 804.
- **Agent** Mr. Stewart, I extended your stay one more night.
- **Guest** Great. By the way, can I request an extra bed in my room?
- **Agent** Let me check the inventory...
  Yes, we have extra rollaway beds available now, sir.
  We can set one up for the additional charge of $20 per night. Would you like to use it?
- **Guest** Yes, please. Thank you for your help.
- **Agent** You're welcome, Mr. Stewart. Have a great day.

❖ Say the following sentences in English.
1. 투숙 기간을 하룻밤 더 연장할 수 있나요?
2. 객실이 비는지 확인해보겠습니다.
3. 투숙 기간을 1박 더 연장해드렸습니다.
4. 제 방에 보조 침대를 요청할 수 있나요?
5. 1박당 추가 요금 20달러에 보조 침대를 설치해드릴 수 있습니다.

Essential Expressions | In-House Guest Service

1. **Telling a guest the opening hours of a hotel's facilities**
   The café serves breakfast from 5:30 A.M. to 10:00 A.M.
   Breakfast will be served from 5:30 A.M. to 10:00 A.M.
   The restaurants stay open until 10:30 P.M.
   The hours of operation are from 7:00 A.M. to 10:00 A.M.

2. **Explaining about additional charges**
   We can set up an extra bed for the additional charge of $20 per night.
   An additional charge will be added to your final bill.
   You'll be charged for late checkout.

Exercises

A Choose the best response to each question.

1. Which of the following does NOT indicate the same thing as the others?
   a. reservation
   b. registration
   c. check-in

2. Which is the main responsibility of a front desk agent?
   a. checking in guests
   b. picking up guests
   c. escorting guests to their rooms

3. Where most likely does a walk-in guest check in to a hotel?
   a. at a hotel front desk
   b. on a hotel's website
   c. at a travel agency

4. Which is NOT necessary to find a guest's reservation?
   a. a confirmation number
   b. the guest's last name
   c. a credit card number

B Match each sentence with the best reply.

1. Under what name is the reservation?
2. Can I extend my stay for another night?
3. Can I check in, please?
4. You reserved a single room for five nights, right?
5. What time is breakfast served?

a. Do you have a reservation with us?
b. Let me check if the room is available.
c. That's correct.
d. You can have breakfast from 6 A.M. to 10 A.M.
e. It's under my name, Larry Wood.

C Complete the following conversation with the words in the box.

> overlooking   imprint   choice   booked   confirmation

Guest: Hello. I would like to check in, please. Here is my 1._____ number.

Receptionist: Thank you. Mr. Miller, you 2._____ a deluxe room for 2 nights and requested a nonsmoking room with an ocean view, but I'm afraid that we don't have any available rooms 3._____ the ocean now. How about a room with the pool view on a high floor instead?

Guest: You leave me no 4._____. I'll take it.

Receptionist: Thank you, Mr. Miller. May I have your credit card to make an 5._____, please?

Guest: Of course. Here you are.

Receptionist: Okay, you are all set.

Role-Playing

A Use the room tariffs below to practice checking in a walk-in guest. Take turns being a receptionist and a guest with your partner.

Room Tariffs

- **Standard Rooms**
  - Deluxe — $200
  - Grand Deluxe — $250

- **Executive Rooms**
  - Deluxe — $300
  - Grand Deluxe — $350

- **Suites**
  - Superior — $500
  - Royal — $800
  - Presidential — $1,000

The above rates are subject to a 10% service charge and a 10% government tax.

Example

- **Receptionist:** Good evening, sir. How may I assist you?
- **Guest:** Do you have any rooms available for tonight?
- **Receptionist:** _____.

B Use the operation hours below to practice telling a guest the hours of operation of the hotel facilities. Take turns being a front desk agent and a guest with your partner.

Operation Hours

- **Basement Floor**
  - Flower Shop — 09:00 A.M. – 08:00 P.M.
  - Drugstore — 07:00 A.M. – 07:00 P.M.

- **Lobby Floor**
  - Coffee Shop — 05:30 A.M. – 11:00 P.M.
  - Lobby Lounge — 06:00 A.M. – 02:00 A.M.
  - Lobby Bar — 06:00 P.M. – 02:00 A.M.

- **2nd Floor**
  - Japanese Restaurant — 12:00 P.M. – 02:30 P.M. / 06:00 P.M. – 10:00 P.M.
  - Chinese Restaurant — 12:00 P.M. – 02:30 P.M. / 06:00 P.M. – 10:00 P.M.
  - Korean Restaurant — 12:00 P.M. – 02:30 P.M. / 06:00 P.M. – 10:00 P.M.

- **3rd Floor**
  - Fitness Club — 05:30 A.M. – 09:30 P.M.

- **5th Floor**
  - Business Center — 07:00 A.M. – 10:00 P.M.

Example

- **Agent:** Good afternoon, sir. May I help you?
- **Guest:** When are the restaurants open?
- **Agent:** _____.

Looking into the Hotel

Read the following passage that describes what the front desk does.

Front Desk

Located in the hotel lobby, the front desk is often considered the most important department in the hotel since it's the place where guests frequently go. Guests approach the front desk in order to check in to and out of a hotel as well as to request information and assistance throughout their stay.

A warm welcome followed by quick and friendly service by the front desk agents can easily make the guests happy. That is why many guests consider them representatives of the hotel. The duties of front desk agents include registering guests, assigning rooms, issuing room keys, exchanging money, providing services for in-house guests, giving information, handling guest complaints, and checking guests out.

The requirements for the front desk agents are the following. First, they must have a positive and cheerful attitude with a smiley face to make any guests feel at ease. Second, they need to be physically healthy and energetic since they stand up during their entire shift. Third, they should be able to communicate well in as many foreign languages as possible, including English. Fourth, some computer skills, such as handling PMS (property management system), are required for this job. Lastly, they must be neat and well-groomed as they contact with guests in person.

Words & Phrases

at ease relaxed
attitude the way you think and feel about something
complaint a statement in which you express your dissatisfaction
in-house guest a guest who is staying at a hotel
issue to publish, release, bring out, or print
lobby a hall near the entrance to a hotel
physically in a way that is related to a person's body
positive hopeful and confident; thinking of the good aspects of a situation rather than the bad ones
representative someone who represents a particular group
request to ask for something politely or formally
well-groomed clean and tidy; well cared for

5

Front Desk II (Cashier)

Unit Objectives
◇ Checkout Service
◇ Handling Disputed Charges & Other Cashiering Services

Warming Up

A Look at the picture below. What is happening? Share your thoughts with your partner.

B Write the correct name of the payment method for each picture.

1 _____   2 _____   3 _____   4 _____

Vocabulary Complete each sentence with the correct word or phrase from the box.

> mistake   remove   look it over   settle   exchange   bill

1. Can you get my _____ ready?
2. Please _____ to see if everything is accurate.
3. I'll _____ that charge from your bill immediately.
4. I'd like to _____ U.S. dollars for Korean currency, please.
5. I apologize for the _____. We will have this resolved as soon as possible.
6. I'm checking out now. I'd like to _____ my bill, please.

Hotel Terminology Learn the following words and phrases used in the hotel industry.

account	an arrangement with a hotel that allows a guest to buy goods now and to pay for them later
audit	an examination of the financial records of a hotel to make sure that they are correct
exchange rate	the rate at which one currency will be exchanged for another
incidental charge	additional charges other than room charges; personal expenses
late checkout	an arrangement that allows guests to check out later than they are supposed to leave
night auditor	an employee in charge of the night audit

Tips to Know

Different Names of Front Desk Agents

Receptionist: a front desk agent who registers guests, assigns rooms, issues keys, and gives guests information during their stays
Cashier: a front desk agent who settles guests' accounts, breaks bills, and changes money for guests
Night Clerk: a front desk agent who handles the work of a receptionist, cashier, and night auditor while working the night (graveyard) shift
Night Auditor: a front desk agent who conducts the night audit while working the night (graveyard) shift

Unit 5 | 59

Conversation 1: Checkout Service

A. Preparing a checkout

05-01

Cashier: Front Desk Cashier

Cashier	Good morning. Front Desk. Carol speaking. How may I assist you?
Guest	Hello. I'm checking out in 10 minutes. Could you send someone up to my room to bring my baggage down to the lobby?[1]
Cashier	Certainly, Mr. Peterson. How many pieces of baggage do you have?
Guest	I have two suitcases, one box, and two bags.
Cashier	Our bellman will be there in a minute with a luggage cart. Is there anything else I can help you with?
Guest	Oh, yes. Could you call a cab to take me to the international airport? How much will the taxi fare be?
Cashier	There should be taxis waiting right outside the door at this time.[2] The fare will be about 80 dollars to the airport depending on traffic.[3]
Guest	Thank you for the information. Could you get my bill ready?[4]
Cashier	Sure, Mr. Peterson. Did you have anything from the minibar since last night?
Guest	Yes. I had one cola and two packages of chocolate chip cookies.
Cashier	Okay, I will add those to your bill. Did you have breakfast at the restaurant this morning?
Guest	No, I didn't. I ordered breakfast from room service.
Cashier	Okay. I will prepare your bill. Please come to the desk when you are ready.

Key & Alternative Expressions

1. **Could you send someone up to my room to bring my baggage down to the lobby?**
   = Can you get someone to bring my baggage down to the lobby?
   = Can you send someone to pick up my luggage?

2. **There should be taxis waiting right outside the door at this time.**
   = There are always taxis outside at this time.

3. **The fare will be about 80 dollars to the airport depending on traffic.**
   = It will cost around 80 dollars to the airport depending on traffic.
   cf. The exact payment will depend on traffic.

4. **Could you get my bill ready?**
   = Could I have my bill, please?
   = Please prepare my bill.
   = Will you make sure my bill is ready, please?

B. Checking out a guest

Cashier: Front Desk Cashier

Guest   Good morning. I'd like to check out, please.

Cashier   Okay. Let me help you with that, sir. What room were you in?

Guest   I was in room 1920. Here is my key.

Cashier   Thank you. Mr. Adams, how was your stay with us?

Guest   It was excellent as always.

Cashier   Did you use the minibar since last night?

Guest   No, I didn't use it at all.

Cashier   Let me print out your bill… It looks like you had breakfast at the café this morning, sir.

Guest   That's right.

Cashier   All right. Here is your bill. Your total is 350,000 won. Please look it over to see if everything is accurate.

❖ Say the following sentences in English.
1. 제가 그것을 도와드리겠습니다.
2. 몇 호실에 투숙하셨습니까?
3. 투숙은 어떠셨습니까?
4. 지난밤 이후로 미니바를 사용하셨습니까?
5. 오늘 아침에 카페에서 조식을 드셨나 보네요.
6. 총금액은 35만원입니다.
7. 모두 정확한지 확인해주시기 바랍니다.

C. Settling a bill

Cashier	Would you like to pay now, Ms. Barnes?
Guest	Yes, please.
Cashier	Are you using the same credit card you gave me when you checked in?
Guest	Actually, can I pay with cash?
Cashier	Of course, ma'am.
Guest	How much do I owe?
Cashier	Your total comes to 220,000 won.
Guest	How much is that in U.S. dollars?
Cashier	It is 183 dollars and 30 cents.
Guest	Here is 200 dollars.
Cashier	Here is your change. It's 20,000 won. Thank you for staying with us, Ms. Barnes. I hope to see you again soon.

Cashier: Front Desk Cashier

❖ **Say the following sentences in English.**

1. 체크인할 때 주신 신용카드를 사용하시겠습니까?
2. 현금으로 결제해도 되나요?
3. 다 해서 22만원 되겠습니다.
4. 미국 달러로는 얼마인가요?
5. 여기 거스름돈입니다. 2만원입니다.

D. Extending the checkout

05-04

Cashier: Front Desk Cashier

Cashier　Good morning. How may I help you?
Guest　Good morning. I'm supposed to leave today, but my flight doesn't depart until late evening. Can I stay in my room until this afternoon? I'm in room 1202.
Cashier　Let me check if the room is available first… Yes, the room is available tonight, Mr. Hunt. You can stay in your room until 6 P.M., but will be charged 50% of the room rate.
Guest　I see. If I check out before noon, can I leave my luggage somewhere in the hotel?
Cashier　Certainly, sir. You can leave your luggage at the bell desk over there. The bellmen will be happy to take care of it for you, sir.
Guest　That's good. I'll do that.
Cashier　Oh, it's almost noon already. If you need some more time to pack your luggage, I can extend your checkout around 30 minutes at no extra charge.
Guest　That sounds perfect! I appreciate it.
Cashier　You're welcome, sir.

❖ Say the following sentences in English.
1　먼저 객실이 비는지 확인해보겠습니다.
2　오후 6시까지 객실에 계실 수 있지만, 객실 요금의 50%가 청구됩니다.
3　정오 전에 체크아웃하면, 호텔 어딘가에 짐을 맡길 수 있나요?
4　짐을 챙기는 데 시간이 좀 더 필요하시면, 체크아웃 시각을 30분 정도 무료로 연장해드릴 수 있습니다.

Essential Expressions | Checkout Service

1. Asking about payment
Are you using the same credit card you gave me when you checked in?
Do you want to charge everything to your Visa card?
Are you paying by credit card?
How would you like to pay (your bill)?

2. Asking if guests enjoyed their stay
How was your stay (with us)?
How did you enjoy your stay (with us)?
Were there any inconveniences during your stay?
Did you enjoy your stay with us?

3. Saying farewell to guests
Thank you for staying with us.
I hope to see you again soon.
We hope you enjoyed your stay here and would be happy to welcome you back soon.
We hope you'll come and stay with us again. Have a safe trip back home.
It was a pleasure having you with us. We look forward to welcoming you again soon.

Unit 5 | 63

Conversation II: Handling Disputed Charges & Other Cashiering Services

A. Handling disputed charges

05-05

Cashier: Front Desk Cashier

Cashier Here is your bill. Please look it over to see if everything is correct.[1]

Guest Oh, thank you. Let me see…
I think there are some mistakes on my bill.[2]
I seem to have been charged for using the minibar, but I didn't take anything from it.

Cashier Let me check the details…
They were a toothbrush, toothpaste, and a razor.

Guest Weren't they complimentary?

Cashier I'm sorry, but we charge for everything inside the minibar. Free toiletries are no longer provided to reduce the use of disposable products. They are included on the price list of the minibar as well.

Guest I see… There is another problem here. This charge from the bar must be wrong. I didn't stop by the bar at all during my stay.

Cashier I'll check the receipt. Please wait a moment… Here it is. Mr. Hill, room 620…

Guest That's neither my name nor my room number. I was in room 1620.

Cashier Yes, you're right. I'm very sorry for the mistake, Mr. Hall.
I'll remove that charge from your bill immediately.[3]

Guest Okay.

Cashier Here is your new bill. Once again, I apologize for the error.

Key & Alternative Expressions

1. Please look it over to see if everything is correct.
= Please have a look at this printout.
= Please check it over to make sure that everything is accurate.

2. I think there are some mistakes on my bill.
= There is something wrong with my bill. = My bill is incorrect. = My bill isn't right.

3. I'll remove that charge from your bill immediately.
= I will deduct that charge from your bill immediately.
= I will adjust your bill immediately.
= I will take that (those) off and make a new bill for you.
cf. I will add that (those) to your bill.

B. Settling an account with a credit card

05-06

Cashier: Front Desk Cashier

Guest   Can I settle my bill now? I'm checking out early tomorrow morning.
Cashier   Certainly. May I have your name and room number, please?
Guest   I'm Tanya Ross in room 1520, and I didn't use the minibar.
Cashier   All right, Ms. Ross. Let me print out your bill... Here you go. Please check it over to make sure everything is correct.
Guest   Okay... It looks right to me.
Cashier   Great. How would you like to pay, ma'am?
Guest   By credit card, please. Here it is.
Cashier   I'm sorry, but your card was declined. Do you have another one?
Guest   Oh, really? Do you take American Express?
Cashier   Yes, we do. We accept all major credit cards.

❖ Say the following sentences in English.
1 모두 맞는지 확인해주시기 바랍니다.
2 결제는 어떻게 하시겠습니까?
3 죄송하지만, 카드 승인이 거절되었습니다. 다른 카드 있으십니까?

C. Exchanging money

05-07

Cashier: Front Desk Cashier

Guest   I'd like to exchange U.S. dollars for Korean currency, please. What's the rate today?
Cashier   Today's exchange rate is 1,100 won to the dollar. How much would you like to change?
Guest   300 dollars, please.
Cashier   How would you like your bills, sir?
Guest   I want some 50,000 won bills and some 10,000 won bills.
Cashier   Very good, sir. May I have your passport and room number, please?

❖ Say the following sentences in English.
1 오늘 환율은 1달러에 1,100원입니다.
2 얼마 환전하시겠습니까?
3 지폐는 어떻게 드릴까요?

D. Handling guest complaints during checkout 05-08

Cashier: Front Desk Cashier

Cashier	Are you leaving one day earlier than expected?
Guest	That's right. My schedule has changed.
Cashier	Your room charge will be put on your company account, Mr. Logan. Here is your itemized bill for the incidental charges.
Guest	Everything looks fine. Here's my credit card.
Cashier	Thank you. How did you enjoy your stay, sir?
Guest	Actually, I was not very satisfied with your hotel this time.
Cashier	I'm sorry to hear that, sir. Were there any problems with your room?
Guest	Because of the noise from the next door, I woke up several times in the middle of the night.
Cashier	Oh, please accept my apologies, Mr. Logan. The guests next door to you were having a bridal shower. I'll put a note in your profile and make sure you get a quieter room the next time you're here.
Guest	Okay, thank you.
Cashier	I assure you it won't happen again on your next visit. If you feel any discomfort during your stay, please let us know at any time. We will take care of it immediately.
Guest	I'll do that. Thank you.

❖ Say the following sentences in English.
1. 예정보다 하루 일찍 떠나십니까?
2. 객실 요금은 고객님의 회사 계좌로 청구될 예정입니다.
3. 여기 부대 비용에 대한 항목별 계산서입니다.
4. 고객 프로필에 메모를 달아두겠습니다.
5. 다음에 방문하시면 이런 일 없을 겁니다.

Essential Expressions | **Handling Disputed Charges & Other Cashiering Services**

1. Telling a guest that a payment failed
I'm sorry, but your card was declined. / This card is not going through.
I'm afraid this card has expired. / I'm afraid this card is no longer valid.
I'm sorry, but this card is over the credit limit. / Your card was declined because you have exceeded your credit limit.

2. Explaining about incidental charges
They were a toothbrush, toothpaste, and a razor.
That's for the room service you ordered for lunch yesterday.
There is an international phone call charge on your bill.
You were charged for two cans of beer.

3. Apologizing politely
I apologize for the error (inconvenience). / Please accept my apology.

Exercises

A Choose the best response to each question.

1. Which is NOT the main responsibility of a front desk agent?
   a. checking out guests
   b. exchanging money
   c. taking breakfast orders

2. Which is NOT necessary to exchange money?
   a. a checkout date
   b. a passport
   c. a room number

3. What does a front desk agent need to check when settling a guest's bill?
   a. the minibar usage of a guest since last night
   b. the plate number of a guest's car
   c. the baggage tag number of a guest

4. What would a front desk agent FIRST say to a guest when he or she complains of a problem with the bill?
   a. We do apologize for our mistakes.
   b. Please have a look at this printout.
   c. Let me check the details.

B Match each sentence with the best reply.

1. How was your stay with us?
2. How much do I owe?
3. Can I leave my luggage somewhere?
4. I think my bill is incorrect.
5. Do you take MasterCard?

a. Your total comes to 200,000 won.
b. Let me check the detailed bill.
c. It was excellent!
d. You may leave it at the bell desk.
e. Yes, we do. We take all major credit cards.

C Complete the following conversation with the words in the box.

| paying | staying | number | check | prepare |

Guest: I'm checking out now. Could you ¹_____ my bill, please?

Cashier: Absolutely, ma'am. May I have your room ²_____, please?

Guest: I was in room 1030. Here is my key. I didn't use the minibar.

Cashier: Here is your bill. Please look it over to ³_____ that everything is correct.

Guest: Everything looks good.

Cashier: How will you be ⁴_____?

Guest: Here is my credit card.

Cashier: Thank you. Please sign here... Here is your receipt. Thank you for ⁵_____ with us.

Role-Playing

Use the guest folio below to practice checking out a guest and handling disputed charges. Take turns being a front desk cashier and a guest with your partner.

Guest Folio

Date	Description	Amount
6/20/19	Room charge	200,000
6/20/19	Room service charge	20,000
6/20/19	Government tax	22,000
6/20/19	Airport pickup service	110,000
6/20/19	Lobby bar	56,000
6/20/19	Korean restaurant	109,000
6/20/19	Pay TV	11,000
6/21/19	Room charge	200,000
6/21/19	Room service charge	20,000
6/21/19	Government tax	22,000
6/21/19	Café	76,000
6/21/19	Chinese restaurant	98,000
6/21/19	Business center	55,000
6/22/19	Airport drop-off service	100,000

Total Due **KW 1,099,000**
Total Paid **KW 0**

Example

Cashier: Good morning, sir. Are you checking out now?
Guest: Yes, I am. Can I see my bill, please?
Cashier: _____.

Looking into the Hotel Read the following passage that describes what the front desk cashier does.

05-09

Front Desk Cashier

The two major jobs of front desk agents are checking guests out (cashiering) and checking guests in (reception). However, no front desk agent is specifically assigned to do either job. Each of the agents at the front desk can be a receptionist or cashier depending on guests' requests. Normally, the checkout time is at noon, and the check-in time is at 3 P.M. Therefore, the morning shift agents usually do cashiering while the afternoon shift agents usually do registration.

If a guest leaves after the checkout time, the hotel usually charges the guest an additional charge for late checkout. The late checkout fee varies from a certain percentage of a room rate to a full charge for a day, depending on the time of the requested late checkout.

Express checkout is a way to check out without stopping by the front desk. Guests can either check their itemized bill by using an on-screen display on an in-room TV, or they can have the bill placed under their door the night before they check out. Guests only have to have left their credit card to make an imprint of it at the front desk when they checked in.

Words & Phrases

assign to give a job
cashier an employee who guests pay money to
charge to ask someone to pay money
display a screen; an arrangement of things that have been put in a particular place
itemized bill a list of charges
job work

major more important, serious, or significant than other things
place to put
shift a particular period of work time during the day or night
stop by to visit a place for a short amount of time
vary to be different

6

Concierge & GRO Desk

Unit Objectives
◇ Concierge Service
◇ GRO (Guest Relations Officer) Service

Warming Up

A Look at the picture below. Who is she? What does she do? Share your thoughts with your partner.

B Choose the picture that is NOT related to a concierge's duties.

a.    b.    c.    d.

Vocabulary Complete each sentence with the correct word or phrase from the box.

| try | interested in | describe | recommend |
| operate | on foot | attending | admission fee |

1. Could you _____ some nice places for shopping?
2. Why don't you _____ our hotel restaurant?
3. It will take about 10 minutes _____.
4. Which conference are you _____?
5. I am _____ Korean history and culture.
6. They _____ from 9 A.M. to 6 P.M.
7. The _____ is included in the ticket price.
8. Can you _____ your lost mobile phone?

Hotel Terminology Learn the following words and phrases used in the hotel industry.

ballroom	a large banquet room used for conferences, wedding ceremonies, and social meetings in a hotel
continental breakfast	a simple breakfast that consists of bread and coffee or tea
corridor	a long passage in a building, especially with rooms on each side
express check-in/checkout	special check-in or checkout service designed for VIP or special request guest
GRO	guest relations officer, usually responsible for VIP guest treatment
Lost & Found	a place where lost property is kept, or the relevant service
video conferencing system	a type of technology that enables people from multiple locations to have a conference without actually meeting in person

Tips to Know

Lost and Found

The lost and found service can be handled by two departments according to the place the lost items were found.

Place Items Were Found	Department in Charge
In a hotel's public areas, such as the lobby, restaurants, or banquet rooms	Concierge
In guest rooms	Housekeeping

Unit 6 | 71

Conversation 1: Concierge Service

A. Recommending tourist attractions

Concierge Good morning, sir. How may I help you?

Guest Hi. This is my first visit to Korea. Could you recommend some famous places to visit in Seoul?[1]

Concierge Well. There are very many popular tourist sites in Seoul. What kind of place would you like to visit?

Guest I'm very interested in Korean history and culture.[2]

Concierge Well… Then you should definitely visit Gyeongbokgung, the main royal palace during the Joseon Dynasty.

Guest Oh, I think I've heard about it before.

Concierge If you want to get a glimpse of Korean traditional life and culture, I would recommend visiting Namsangol Hanok Village.[3] You can actually learn all about Korean culture there. For instance, you can try *hanbok*, Korean traditional clothes, learn Hangeul calligraphy, the Korean alphabet, and take Korean traditional etiquette classes such as the tea ceremony. You can also try traditional games and take a guided tour of the hanok village area.

Guest Both places sound like a lot of fun! I'm really looking forward to visiting them.

Concierge For your information, those two places are close to each other. It only takes about 10 minutes by taxi from the palace to the hanok village.

Guest Excellent! How much is the admission fee at each place?

Concierge The entrance fee for Gyeongbokgung is 3,000 won, and the hanok village has no entrance fee.

Key & Alternative Expressions

1. **Could you recommend some famous places to visit in Seoul?**
   = Can you suggest some nice places in Seoul?
   = Can you give me some advice for traveling Seoul?

2. **I'm very interested in Korean history and culture.**
   = I have interest in your history and culture.
   = I'm curious to know about Korean history and culture.

3. **I would recommend visiting Namsangol Hanok Village.**
   = Why don't you visiting Namsangol Hanok Village?
   = How about visiting Namsangol Hanok Village?
   = You should definitely visit Namsangol Hanok Village.
   = I suggest visiting Namsangol Hanok Village.
   = I suggest you visit Namsangol Hanok Village.
   = You can't miss Namsangol Hanok Village.

B. Recommending restaurants

06-02

Guest — I'd like to have some Korean food. Can you recommend a good restaurant?
Concierge — We have a Korean restaurant on the 2nd floor. It has some good authentic Korean food.
Guest — I've already been there. I want to try another place this time.
Concierge — In that case, there is a place called Hansarang near the hotel. It's only a 10-minute walk from here. And there is another restaurant called K-Garden. It'll take about 20 minutes by taxi to get there. They both operate from 11 A.M. to 11 P.M.
Guest — How is the food at each place?
Concierge — The food at both places is great. But the menus are a little different. Hansarang is an authentic Korean food restaurant while K-Garden is famous for its meat dishes such as *bulgogi* and *galbi*. If you love meat, I would recommend K-Garden. You can also enjoy shopping after lunch. The restaurant is located on Garosu-gil, and the area has many trendy stores and open-air cafés.
Guest — Oh, that's nice. Then I will choose K-Garden.
Concierge — Would you like me to make a reservation for you?
Guest — That would be wonderful.

❖ Say the following sentences in English.
1 여기서 걸어서 10분 거리밖에 안 됩니다.
2 제가 예약을 해드릴까요?

C. Locating lost items

06-03

Guest — Excuse me, but I lost my wallet somewhere in the lobby. Who should I talk to?
Concierge — I can help you with that, sir. When did you lose it?
Guest — Just now, I guess. I was in the lobby about an hour ago, and then I went to the coffee shop to meet my friend. When I met him, I realized I didn't have my wallet in my pocket.
Concierge — I'm sorry to hear that, sir. Can you describe what it looks like?
Guest — It is a brown leather wallet. It has a big letter B on the front.
Concierge — All right. Let me check the list of lost items, sir... Oh, here it is. Let me get it from the back.
Guest — Oh, thank you very much.
Concierge — My pleasure.

❖ Say the following sentences in English.
1 어떻게 생겼는지 설명해주시겠습니까?
2 뒤에서 그것을 가져오겠습니다.

D. Giving advice & directions for shopping

06-04

Guest I need to buy some souvenirs for my family. I also want to visit a Korean traditional market. Is there any place I can do both?

Concierge Of course, ma'am. There are Namdaemun Market and Dongdaemun Market. They are two of the biggest traditional markets in Seoul.

Guest So... Are they pretty much the same?

Concierge Not really, ma'am. Namdaemun Market is more traditional than Dongdaemun Market. There are many street vendors at Namdaemun Market while there are many modern shopping malls at Dongdaemun Market.

Guest I want to visit both of them. Can I visit them by subway? I really want to take the subway in Seoul.

Concierge Certainly. Here is a map of Seoul. A subway map is on the back. You are here, and Dongdaemun Market is right here at Dongdaemun History & Culture Park Station. Turn left as soon as you go through the hotel's revolving door, and walk straight for about 5 minutes. You'll see the subway station right in front of you.

❖ Say the following sentences in English.
1 가족에게 줄 기념품을 좀 사야 합니다.
2 남대문시장에는 노점상이 많은 반면, 동대문시장에는 현대적인 쇼핑몰이 많습니다.
3 호텔 회전문을 통과하시자마자 좌회전하셔서 5분 정도 직진하십시오.
4 바로 앞에 지하철역이 보이실 겁니다.

Essential Expressions | Concierge Service

1. Asking a guest's interests
What kind of place would you like to visit?
What are you interested in?
Do you have any particular place in mind?

2. Telling the distance and time required to get to a destination
It's (only) a 10-minute walk from here.
It takes about 15 minutes on foot.
It takes about 20 minutes by walking.
I'll take about 5 minutes by car.
It is within walking distance. / It's a bit far.

Conversation II — GRO (Guest Relations Officer) Service

A. Checking in VIP guests

(A VIP guest's car arrives at the hotel.)

GRO Welcome back, Ms. Lane. I'm Gary, a GRO. Let me escort you to your room.[1] Your luggage will be delivered to your room shortly.

Guest Thank you. Your service is excellent as always.[2]

GRO My pleasure, Ms. Lane. This way, please...

(In the elevator...)

GRO We've given you a room on the 15th floor as usual.

Guest Oh, you remembered that is my favorite floor. Did you set up a laptop in my room?

GRO Absolutely, Ms. Lane. We also set up a printer according to your request.

Guest Thank you.

(Both get off the elevator.)

GRO Here we are. After you, Ms. Lane. Your room is on the right. This is your room.

(They open the door and go in.)

GRO *(After showing the room to the guest)* Here is your room key. Do you need anything else?

Guest Not right now. Thank you.

GRO Very good, Ms. Lane. Please dial 101 on your room phone if you need anything.[3] You'll be able to reach the guest relations officer desk any time from 7 A.M. to 10 P.M.

Key & Alternative Expressions

1. **Let me escort you to your room.**
   = I'll take you to your room.
   = Let me walk you to your room.
   = I'll show you to your room.

2. **Your service is excellent as always.**
   = Your service is excellent as usual.
   = I'm always pleased with your service.

3. **Please dial 101 on your room phone if you need anything.**
   = Please call me if you need me.
   = Please let us (me) know if you need anything.
   = Please do not hesitate to contact us if you need any further assistance.
   = Please feel free to contact me if you have any futher questions.

B. Handling requests from a VIP guest

GRO Thank you for calling. This is GRO. Amanda speaking. How may I assist you?

Guest Hi, Amanda. I'm Greg Simmons in room 1512. I'd like to book a conference room for tomorrow.

GRO Okay… Could you give me some details, please?

Guest I'll need a conference room equipped with a videoconferencing system at 7:00 tomorrow morning. Five people will attend the conference. If we could, we would like to have breakfast while we have the conference.

GRO We can do that for you, Mr. Simmons. What would you like to order for breakfast?

Guest A continental breakfast for five will do. Please make sure that there are toast, orange juice, and coffee.

GRO I see. I'll arrange a video conference for 7 o'clock tomorrow morning with five continental breakfasts. Do you have anything else to request?

Guest No, that's it for now.

GRO All right, Mr. Simmons. Please let me know if you have any further requests.

❖ Say the following sentences in English.
1. 자세한 사항을 말씀해주시겠습니까?
2. 내일 아침 7시에 화상 회의 설비를 갖춘 회의실이 필요합니다.
3. 토스트, 오렌지 주스, 커피를 반드시 준비해주십시오.
4. 내일 아침 7시 정각에 화상 회의와 유럽식 조식 5인분을 준비해놓겠습니다.
5. 그 밖에 더 요청하실 것이 있으면 알려주십시오.

C. Giving directions to hotel facilities

Guest Pardon me. I'm here to attend a conference. Where is the conference room?

GRO Which conference are you attending, ma'am? We have many different conferences taking place now.

Guest Here is my invitation.

GRO Let me see… Your conference will be held in the grand ballroom on the 2nd floor. It is scheduled to start at 2 P.M. You can take the escalator on your left. You may also take the stairs or elevator on your right.

Guest Thank you. By the way, where is the restroom?

GRO Go straight toward the coffee shop. Then, turn right and go to the end of the hall. The restroom will be on your left. You can't miss it.

❖ Say the following sentences in English.
1 고객님의 회의는 2층 그랜드볼룸에서 열립니다.
2 회의는 오후 2시에 시작할 예정입니다.
3 커피숍 쪽으로 직진하십시오.
4 우회전하셔서 복도 끝까지 가십시오.
5 찾기 쉬우실 겁니다.

D. Saying farewell to a guest 06-08

(A GRO approaches a guest checking out with a friendly smile.)

GRO Good morning, sir. Are you leaving now?
Guest Yes, I am.
GRO You can check out over here. Come this way, please...
Guest Okay.
GRO How was your stay, sir?
Guest Well, everything was excellent, except for one thing.
GRO What was the problem, sir?
Guest My room was really cold. I tried to adjust the temperature and got an extra blanket, but the room was still freezing.
GRO I apologize for the inconvenience.
The rooms located on both ends of the corridor tend to be colder than the others.
I'll put a note on your profile so that you can get a room in the middle on your next visit.
Guest Thank you.
GRO Are you going to Incheon International Airport?
Guest Yes, I am.
GRO Do you have transportation to the airport?
Guest I'm going to take a taxi.
GRO Let me arrange a taxi and have a bellman put your baggage into the trunk while you settle the bill.
Guest That would be nice. Thank you very much.
GRO We hope you come and stay with us again. Have a safe trip back home, sir.

❖ **Say the following sentences in English.**
1. 복도 양 끝에 위치한 객실이 다른 객실보다 추운 경향이 있습니다.
2. 제가 고객 프로파일에 메모를 달아서 다음번 방문하실 때는 중앙에 있는 객실을 배정받으실 수 있도록 하겠습니다.
3. 고객님께서 정산하시는 동안, 택시를 준비하고 벨맨을 시켜 짐을 트렁크에 넣겠습니다.

Essential Expressions | **GRO (Guest Relations Officer) Service**

1. Saying that a service will be ready
I'll arrange a video conference. / I'll prepare eight continental breakfasts.
I'll organize personal training sessions in the fitness club. / I'll book a dinner reservation for you.

2. Promising guests better services on their next visit
I'll put a note on your profile so that you can get a room in the middle on your next visit.
I'll leave a note in your profile for my colleagues to double-check the smell in your room on your next stay.
I'll make sure to put a note on your profile to avoid a squeaky bed in the future.
I'll make a note in your profile that you prefer a quieter room.

Exercises

A Choose the best response to each question.

1. Which department does a concierge belong to?
   a. Food & Beverage
   b. Rooms
   c. Back Office

2. Who is in charge of taking care of VIP guests and handling their complaints?
   a. a concierge
   b. a cashier
   c. a GRO

3. Who is in charge of express check-in service for VIP guests?
   a. a front desk agent
   b. a bellhop
   c. a GRO

4. Which is NOT a duty of a concierge?
   a. exchanging foreign currency
   b. advising guests about tour programs
   c. handling lost and found items

B Match each sentence with the best reply.

1. What are you interested in?
2. How much is the admission fee?
3. How long does it take?
4. Do you have anything else to request?
5. How was your stay?

a. I'm interested in art and music.
b. It takes about 10 minutes by car.
c. That's it for now.
d. Everything was excellent!
e. It's free.

C Complete the following conversation with the words in the box.

| floor | advice | admission | open | visit |

Concierge Good morning, ma'am. How may I assist you?

Guest Hello. I'd like to do some sightseeing in Seoul. Could you give me some ¹_____?

Concierge N Seoul Tower is a nice place to ²_____. It is located at the top of Mt. Namsan. It has an observatory on the third ³_____. You can enjoy great panoramic views of the city up there.

Guest That sounds wonderful! When is the observatory ⁴_____?

Concierge The observatory deck is open from 10 A.M. to 11 P.M. The ⁵_____ fee is 10,000 won.

Role-Playing

Use the floor plan of a hotel below to practice giving directions to a guest. Take turns being a GRO and a guest with your partner. Use the expressions in the box if needed.

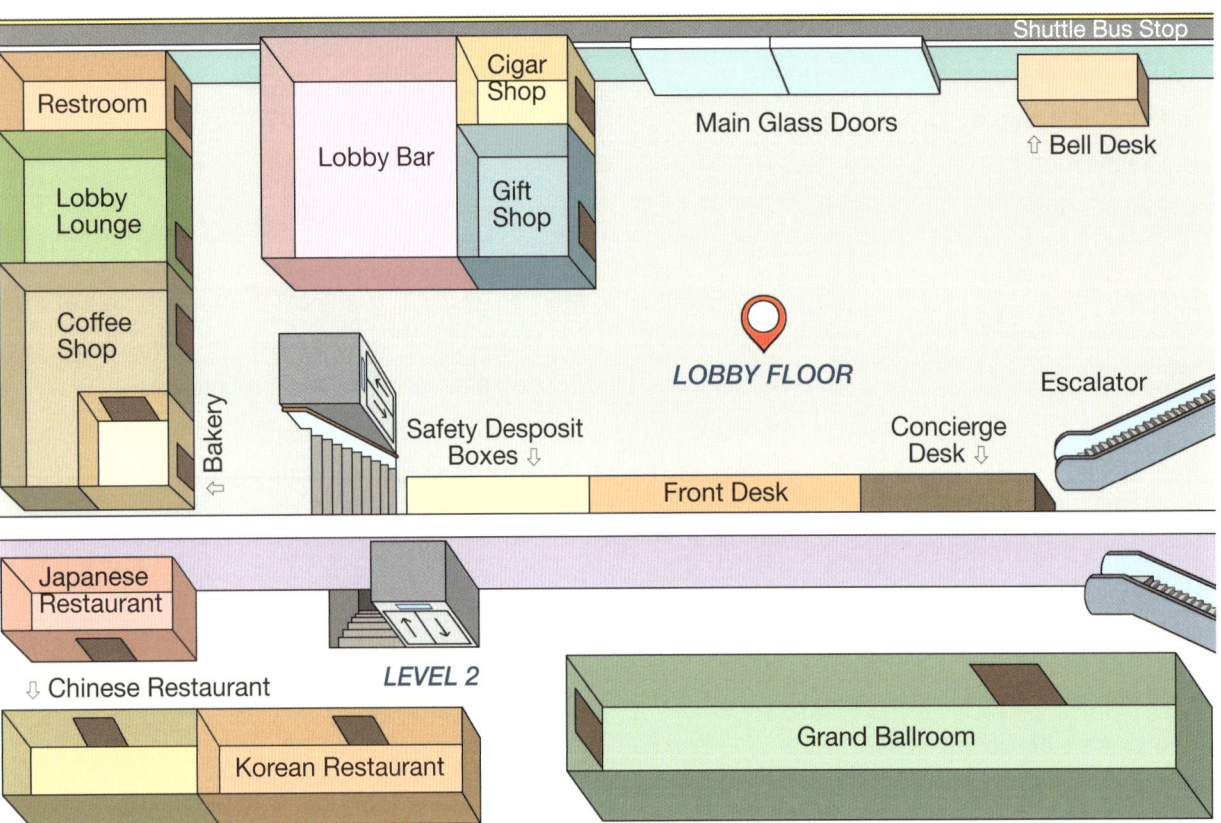

Example

GRO Good afternoon, ma'am. May I help you?
Guest Yes. Where is the Korean restaurant?
GRO Take the elevator over there to the 2nd floor. When you get out, you will see the Korean restaurant in front of you.

Giving Directions

_____ is **over there**.

Go straight toward _____.

Go between _____ **and** _____.

Go down the hallway **until you see** _____ on your left.

Walk straight down this corridor. It will be on your right.

Walk along this corridor and **take the first left**.

Walk down the hallway and turn right **after** _____.

Keep walking to _____, and then turn right.

When you come to _____, turn left.

You'll find _____ on the right, **just past/before** _____.

_____ is **at the end of** the hallway on the left.

It's **on** the _____ floor.

Go upstairs / downstairs.

Take the elevator / escalator **to** the _____ floor.

When you **go out of** the elevator, _____.

When you **get out**, _____.

From _____, **walk across** the lobby.

Walk through the doors and then immediately turn left.

It is **straight ahead of** you.

It is **in front of / opposite / next to / behind** _____.

Looking into the Hotel

Read the following passage that describes what the concierge and GRO do.

Concierges and GROs

A concierge assists guests with almost everything throughout their stays. He recommends local attractions, shopping places, restaurants, and transportation. He makes booking arrangements as well. He not only makes reservations for restaurants, sightseeing tours, and transportation for guests, but he also books tickets for plays, sporting events, and any other activities they want to do. Since a concierge is frequently asked questions about the area's best spots, history, and culture, he has to be knowledgeable about the city where the hotel is located. A concierge also handles inquiries regarding lost and found items and lends guests wheelchairs and strollers.

While one of the main responsibilities of a concierge is to provide guests with information about the hotel's facilities and services as well as local travel for guests, the most important duty of a GRO is to serve VIP guests. A GRO performs express check-in and secretarial services for VIP guests during their stays. A GRO also handles all types of requests, questions, and complaints from guests as a one-stop service. In addition, a GRO stands by in the lobby to welcome arriving guests and says farewell to departing guests. When the hotel is very busy, a GRO even supports his colleagues from other departments such as the front desk, concierge desk, and the Executive Floor Department.

A hotel concierge and a GRO must be fit, stay cheerful and patient, have good manners, and be fluent in as many foreign languages as possible in order to act as a qualified personal assistant to the guests.

Words & Phrases

arrangement plans or preparations to make something happen
assist to help someone by doing something for that person
cheerful friendly and pleasant in behavior
knowledgeable knowing a lot about something
lend to give something for a short time, expecting it to be given back
patient able to wait a long time

perform to do something
recommend to suggest that something is good or useful
regarding about; concerning
secretarial relating to the work of a secretary
sightseeing traveling to interesting places that tourists usually visit
stroller a small chair on wheels in which a baby or small child can sit and be wheeled around

7
Executive Floor

Warming Up

A Look at the picture below. Have you ever heard about executive floors in a hotel? What do you know about them? Share your thoughts with your partner.

B What does the room rate for executive floors usually include? Check the correct boxes.

a. breakfast	☐	b. meeting room	☐
c. dinner	☐	d. happy hour	☐
e. late checkout after 6 P.M.	☐	f. fitness center	☐

Vocabulary Complete each sentence with the correct word or phrase from the box.

| all-day | explain | business card | separate |
| take a seat | access | billed | along with |

1 Why don't you _____ while I check you in?
2 I'll need your _____ to register your information.
3 Can you _____ the benefits of staying on an executive club floor?
4 The executive lounge serves _____ complimentary refreshments.
5 You can enjoy exclusive _____ to the executive lounge.
6 Can you split the bill into two _____ ones?
7 Complimentary breakfast is served in the executive lounge _____ soft drinks and snacks.
8 I ordered room service and had it _____ to my room.

Hotel Terminology Learn the following words and phrases used in the hotel industry.

executive floor — a special floor at a hotel; club floor; club level; business floor

happy hour — an EFL service; a period of the day when guests can have unlimited alcoholic beverages along with some finger foods and snacks (usually in the evening)

Tips to Know

The Key Services of Executive Floor Lounges
- Executive lounge express check-in and checkout service
- Free Internet access
- Complimentary breakfast
- All-day complimentary coffee and tea
- Complimentary alcoholic beverages, hors d'oeuvres, finger foods, and snacks during happy hour
- Free use of meeting rooms (Free hours may vary depends on hotels.)
- Complimentary ironing service (1-2 pieces)
- Shoeshine service
- Newspaper delivery service
- Complimentary access to the fitness center: gym, indoor swimming pool, and sauna

Unit 7 | 83

Conversation 1: EFL Check-In & Checkout Service

A. EFL check-in service

Agent: Executive Floor Guest Service Agent

Agent Good morning. Welcome to the Crimson Hotel. May I assist you?

Guest Yes, I'm checking in.[1] My name is Luis Howard.

Agent Sure, Mr. Howard. Would you please take a seat?[2]
Okay… You have a reservation for three nights in an executive deluxe room with a double bed. Is that correct?

Guest That's right. I'll be checking out on Saturday.

Agent May I have your business card so that I can register your information?

Guest No problem. Here you are.

Agent How would you like to pay?

Guest With my VISA card.

Agent May I have your credit card to make an imprint?

Guest Sure, here it is.

Agent What time do you expect to check out on Saturday, sir?

Guest Um… I'm thinking of checking out at around 2:30 P.M.

Agent Let me extend your checkout time then.
Will you need transportation to the airport?

Guest Yes. Can you arrange it, please?

Agent Sure. Could you tell me your departure time and the flight number, please?

Guest It's at 5:30 P.M. I'll be on flight OZ123 departing from Incheon International Airport.

Agent I see. I'll arrange a limousine to the airport. The fee will be billed to your room. You're all set, Mr. Howard. Here is your room key. Your room is on the 17th floor. Let me briefly explain about our EFL services. You can enjoy all-day refreshments in the lounge until 10 P.M. Happy hour runs from 5 P.M. to 8 P.M. Breakfast is served from 6:30 A.M. to 10:00 A.M. The meeting room is available for up to 2 hours a day. In addition, you have free access to our fitness center, which has a pool. May I have your luggage tag? I'll have your bags delivered to your room.

Guest Here you go.

Agent Enjoy your stay, Mr. Howard.

Key & Alternative Expressions

1. I am checking in.
= I am going to check in. = I will be checking in. = I would like to check in. = I'm ready to check in.

2. Would you please take a seat?
= Please have a seat so that I can register your information. = Would you please have a seat (while I check you in)?

B. EFL checkout service

07-02

Agent: Executive Floor Guest Service Agent

Agent   Good morning, Mr. Parker. Are you checking out?

Guest   Yes. Can you prepare my bill while I am having breakfast?
Here is my key. I took one beer from the minibar.

Agent   Of course. Do you need assistance with your luggage?

Guest   Yes, that would be great.

Agent   Oh, you reserved a limousine to the airport for 10 A.M. I will get your limo ready and have a bellman bring your baggage down to the car. Enjoy your breakfast, Mr. Parker.

(15 minutes later…)

Guest   Is my bill ready?

Agent   Yes, Mr. Parker. Here is your bill. Please look it over to see if everything is correct.

Guest   Everything looks fine. Can you make two separate bills for me?
My company will only pay for the room, and I will take care of the rest.

Agent   Certainly, Mr. Parker. Here they are.

Guest   Perfect. I'll pay with my AMEX card.

Agent   Okay, Mr. Parker. You are all set. Here are your separate bills and the receipts.
Your luggage is already loaded in the limousine out front.

(The agent walks the guest to an elevator and presses the button to go down.)

Agent   How was your stay, Mr. Parker?

Guest   Oh, it was excellent as usual.

Agent   I'm very pleased to hear that.

(The elevator doors finally open, and the guest gets in.)

Agent   Have a nice trip back home, Mr. Parker.
We're looking forward to seeing you again soon.

❖ Say the following sentences in English.
1. 제가 조식을 먹을 동안 계산서를 준비해주실 수 있습니까?
2. 계산서를 두 개로 나누어주실 수 있습니까?
3. 리무진을 대기시키고 벨맨을 시켜 짐을 차 있는 곳까지 내려드리겠습니다.

Essential Expressions | EFL Check-In & Checkout Service

1. Offering to help a checking-out guest
Do you need assistance with your luggage?
Would you like me to arrange transportation for you?

2. Helping a guest checking out with baggage and transportation
I will get your limo ready and have a bellman bring your baggage down to the car.
Let me have a cab waiting outside for you.

Conversation II: Lounge & Meeting Room Service

A. EFL lounge service

07-03

Agent: Executive Floor Guest Service Agent

When a guest comes in after the breakfast hours

- **Guest** Can I have breakfast now?
- **Agent** I'm sorry, but the breakfast hours are over.[1]
- **Guest** What are the breakfast hours?[2]
- **Agent** Breakfast is from 6 A.M. to 10 A.M., ma'am.
- **Guest** Oh, I woke up late this morning. What can I do?
- **Agent** You can still order a continental breakfast by calling room service until 11 A.M. I can place an order for you if you want, ma'am.
- **Guest** That would be wonderful!

When a guest orders an alcoholic beverage after happy hour

- **Agent** Would you like to order something to drink, sir?
- **Guest** Yes. Can I have a glass of red wine, please? It's free, right?
- **Agent** I'm sorry, but alcoholic beverages are free of charge only during happy hour. If you would like to order one now, it will be charged to your room. Will that be all right, sir?
- **Guest** Oh, I didn't realize how late it was.[3] I'll just have a cola with ice.

Key & Alternative Expressions

1. I'm sorry, but the breakfast hours are over.
= I'm afraid that the breakfast hours are finished.

2. What are the breakfast hours?
= What time is breakfast served?
= What time does breakfast begin?
= What time does breakfast end?

3. I didn't realize how late it was.
= I totally lost of time.
= Oh, gosh, look at the time.
= My, how time flies!

B. EFL meeting room service

Guest	I'd like to reserve a meeting room, please.
Agent	Sure. When would you like to use it?
Guest	I need it tomorrow from 1 P.M. to 4 P.M.
Agent	All right, ma'am. Please wait a moment while I check… Yes, it's available at that time. May I have your room number, please?
Guest	I'm staying in room 1816.
Agent	How many people will be using the meeting room?
Guest	There will be five people in total, including two from other hotels.
Agent	The meeting room is available free of charge for two hours per room. So you can use it for the entire 3 hours at no extra charge if you have another EFL guest in your group. Can you give me another person's name, Ms. Green?
Guest	Mr. Brandon Young is in our group, but I don't remember his room number.
Agent	No problem. Let me check for you… Okay, he is one of our executive guests. Is there anything else you need in the meeting room?
Guest	Yes, we would like to have the meeting over lunch. Can we order 5 club sandwiches and coffees, please? And charge everything to my room, please.
Agent	All right, ma'am. Will that be all?
Guest	Yes, that's it for now.
Agent	Thank you, Ms. Green. If you need anything else, please contact us on the executive floor.

Agent: Executive Floor Guest Service Agent

❖ Say the following sentences in English.
1 회의실을 예약하고 싶은데요.
2 언제 이용하려고 하십니까?
3 그때 이용하실 수 있습니다.
4 몇 분이 회의실을 이용하실 예정입니까?
5 회의실은 객실 하나당 2시간씩 무료로 이용하실 수 있습니다.
6 다른 분 성함을 말씀해주시겠습니까?
7 더 필요한 것이 있으시면, 비지니스 전용층으로 연락 주십시오.

Essential Expressions | Lounge & Meeting Room Service

1. Asking the number of group members

How many people will be using the meeting room?
How many people will be coming?
How many people will be attending the meeting?
How many people are there in your group?
How large is your party?
How many are you?
May I have the number of guests?

2. Asking if there are any additional requests

Will that be all?
Is there anything else you need?
Is that everything?

3. Telling guests what to do if they need additional requests

If you need anything else, please contact us on the executive floor.
If you'd like to change your reservation, please give us a call.
If you need any other assistance, please call us at any time.
Let me know if there is anything else I can do for you.

Exercises

A Choose the best response to each question.

1. What does the EFL stand for?
   a. excellent floor lounge
   b. executive floor lounge
   c. extended floor lounge

2. When are alcoholic beverages free in the EFL?
   a. during happy hour
   b. during breakfast hours
   c. all day

3. Which department does the EFL most resemble?
   a. bell desk
   b. food and beverage
   c. front desk

4. What information do you need to reserve an EFL meeting room?
   a. a guest's age
   b. a guest's room number
   c. a guest's credit card number

B Match each sentence with the best reply.

1. Is my bill ready?
2. What time do you expect to check out on Monday?
3. How many people are there in your group?
4. Do you need a limousine to the airport?
5. Can you split the bill?

a. I will be checking out at 10:30 A.M.
b. That's not a problem.
c. There will be six of us.
d. Yes. Can you arrange that for me?
e. Sure. Please take a seat so that we can settle your bill.

C Complete the following conversation with the words in the box.

> free of charge   hours   place an order   refreshments   finished

Guest: Hi. I'm here to have breakfast.

Agent: I'm very sorry, sir. The breakfast ¹_____ are ²_____. Breakfast is from 6 A.M. to 10 A.M.

Guest: Oh, that's too bad. Maybe I should just stuff myself with some ³_____. They are ⁴_____, right?

Agent: Don't worry, sir. You can still have a continental breakfast by ordering room service. Would you like me to ⁵_____ for you?

Guest: That sounds perfect!

Role-Playing

A Practice checking in an executive floor guest. Take turns being a guest service agent and a guest with your partner.

Example

Agent   Good morning, ma'am. How may I assist you?
Guest   I would like to check in, please.
Agent   _____.

B Practice assisting an executive floor guest who wants to use the meeting room. Take turns being a guest service agent and a guest with your partner.

Example

Agent   Good afternoon, sir. How may I help you?
Guest   Can I reserve a meeting room?
Agent   _____.

Looking into the Hotel Read the following passage that describes what the executive floor lounge is.

Executive Floor Lounge (EFL)

Most of the upscale hotels located in downtown areas have an executive floor. An executive floor is also called a club floor, club lounge, business floor, or business club by hotels. Hotels designate a certain floor, usually an upper one, as the executive floor and place a private lounge on it to serve special guests. The executive floor is often described as "a hotel within a hotel." The reason is that an EFL offers almost everything that business travelers need during their stays along with a well-appointed exclusive lounge environment. These guests are mostly businessmen or VIP guests staying on the executive floor or in suites.

The executive floor lounge usually opens from 6:30 A.M. to 10:00 P.M. During the hours of operation, guests can experience private express check-in and checkout, have breakfast, and enjoy happy hour in the club lounge. In addition, they can use the meeting room next to the lounge for relaxation or meetings.

The executive floor guest service agents always stand by in the lounge so that guests can ask questions and make requests at their convenience. At some hotels, this is called butler service. This service allows executive floor guests to have their own secretaries during their stays. Since many EFL guests are repeat guests, it is very important for the EFL team to have good relationships with them and to make sure they feel comfortable.

As an EFL guest service agent, you have to be fluent in foreign languages, including English, be sociable, be well aware of global etiquette, be friendly, and always be ready to attend to the individual needs of the guests.

Words & Phrases

butler service a special service to meet an individual guest's every need
designate to set aside for a particular purpose
exclusive available only to a particular group; limited to special people
relationship a bond; a connection
repeat guest a regular guest
secretary a person who is employed to do office work
sociable friendly and fond of talking to other people
upscale designed for people who have a lot of money
well-appointed having all the necessary furniture or equipment

8

Housekeeping

Unit Objectives
◊ Making up Rooms
◊ Other Housekeeping Services

Warming Up

A Look at the picture below. Who is most likely to use this type of cart? What sort of items are inside? Share your thoughts with your partner.

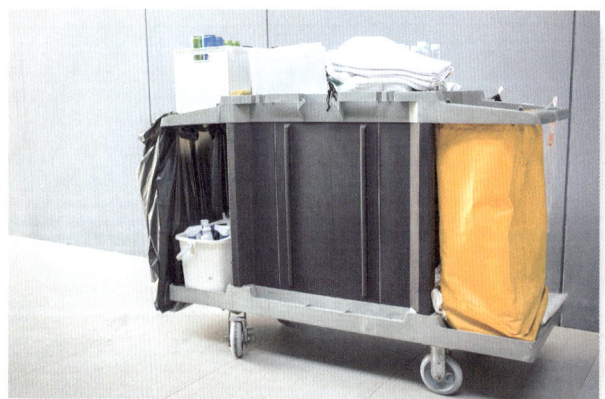

B Write the correct name for each item.

sewing kit   bandage   toilet paper   multi-adaptor

1. _____ 2. _____ 3. _____ 4. _____

Vocabulary Complete each sentence with the correct word or phrase from the box.

| come in | allergic to | stain |
| out of order | hang up | deliver |

1. The air conditioner is _____.
2. I am _____ feathers.
3. Housekeeping. May I _____?
4. We will pick up and _____ your laundry to your room.
5. You can _____ the "Do Not Disturb" sign on the door.
6. Can you remove this tomato sauce _____ from my sweater?

Hotel Terminology Learn the following words and phrases used in the hotel industry.

"Do Not Disturb" sign	a sign that hotel guests can put on the door to inform the hotel staff that they don't want to be interrupted
houseman	an employee who keeps guest rooms and common areas in a hotel clean and delivers amenities to guest rooms
laundry slip	a paper that a guest fills out and hands in to a housekeeping staff member when requesting laundry service
make up a room	to clean up a room by putting things in order and changing the linens
"Make up Room" sign	a sign that hotel guests can put on the door to inform the hotel staff that they want their rooms to be cleaned
room attendant	an employee who cleans guest rooms at a hotel; a room maid
turndown service	a service in which a room attendant goes into guest rooms in the early evening to tidy them up, to turn the sheets down, and sometimes to leave a mint or chocolate on a pillow prior to bedtime

Tips to Know

Hotels Going Green

More and more hotels are choosing to help the environment. By doing so, they can both minimize the impact on Earth and also save hotels large amounts of water, energy, and money. There are many environmentally friendly practices that hotels carry out. For instance, some hotels put table brochures, door hangers, or pillow cards in hotel rooms to encourage their guests to reuse their towels and sheets more than once. The decision is up to the guests, but many of them are glad to participate in this kind of green campaign.

Conversation 1: Making up Rooms

A. "Make up Room" service 08-01

Attendant: Room Attendant

Attendant Housekeeping. Hello? May I come in?[1]
Guest Yes? What's the matter?
Attendant May I come in to make up your room, sir?
Guest Well... Could you come back later?[2]
Attendant Sure, sir. I'm sorry to disturb you.
Please hang up the "Do Not Disturb" sign next time.
Then, you won't be disturbed, sir.
Guest Okay, I will. Oh, can I get two face towels now?
Attendant Sure. Here you are. When you need your room cleaned, please hang up the "Make up Room" sign or call the operator.
Guest Okay, thank you.
(A few hours later...)

Attendant Housekeeping.
Guest Please come in.
Attendant You hung up the "Make up Room" sign, didn't you?
Guest That's right.
Attendant May I clean up your room now?
Guest Yes, you may. How long will it take?
Attendant It'll only take about 15 to 20 minutes, sir.
Guest All right. Go ahead. I'll come back in 20 minutes.

Key & Alternative Expressions

1. Housekeeping. Hello? May I come in?
 = Excuse me, sir. I'm a room attendant. Do you mind if I come in?
 = Good morning, sir. It's a room maid. Can I come in?
 = Room maid. Is anyone here? May I come in?

2. Could you come back later?
 = Could you come back another time?
 cf. Could you come back in another hour?
  Could you come back in two hours?

B. Handling "Make up Room" service requests

08-02

Operator   Good afternoon, Ms. Daniels. How may I assist you?
Guest   Can you send someone to make up my room?
Operator   Certainly, ma'am.
           A maid will be there right away.
           Is there anything else you need?
Guest   I'd like an extra blanket. Can you also send me an iron and ironing board?
Operator   Absolutely, ma'am.
           I'll have a maid bring them to you.
Guest   That's so kind of you.
Operator   Thank you, Ms. Daniels.

❖ Say the following sentences in English.
  1 객실을 정비해주실 분 좀 보내주시겠습니까?
  2 객실정비원이 곧 그곳으로 갈 것입니다.
  3 다리미와 다리미판도 보내주시겠어요?
  4 객실정비원을 시켜 가져다드리겠습니다.
  5 참 친절하시군요.

C. Handling a turndown service request 08-03

Operator	Good evening, Mr. Adams. How may I assist you?
Guest	I forgot to take off the "Do Not Disturb" sign. Can I get turndown service now?
Operator	Sure. Is there anything else you need?
Guest	Yes. Can you change my pillow? I am allergic to feathers.
Operator	Of course, sir. I will send someone with a nonallergenic foam pillow right away.
Guest	That sounds great. Oh, there is one more thing. The TV seems out of order.
Operator	I'm very sorry about that, Mr. Adams. I'll send a maintenance man to your room right away.

❖ Say the following sentences in English.
1 깜빡하고 '방해 금지' 표지를 뗀다는 걸 잊었네요.
2 지금 객실 정돈 서비스를 받을 수 있나요?
3 저는 깃털 알레르기가 있습니다.
4 직원을 시켜 즉시 알레르기 방지 폼 베개를 올려보내겠습니다.
5 지금 바로 시설팀 직원을 객실로 보내겠습니다.

Essential Expressions | **Making up Rooms**

1. After making up guest rooms
I'm sorry for disturbing you. Have a nice day.
Please forgive me for interrupting you. Have a great evening.
Please excuse me for bothering you. Have a good night.

2. Telling a guest that a request will be met
A maid will be there right away.
I'll have a maid bring them to you.
I'll send someone with a nonallergenic foam pillow right away.
I'll send a maintenance man to your room as soon as possible.
I will have it fixed immediately.
Someone will be there to fix your toilet shortly.

Conversation II — Other Housekeeping Services

A. Laundry service

Attendant: Laundry Attendant

Operator: Good afternoon, Ms. Carson. How may I assist you?

Guest: Hello. I have some laundry. Can you send someone to pick them up?

Operator: All right, ma'am. I will send someone up to your room right away.

(A few minutes later…)

Attendant: Good morning, ma'am. I'm here to pick up your laundry.

Guest: Here you go. This dress needs dry cleaning.[1] There is a wine stain on a sleeve. Do you think it will come out?

Attendant: Well… We cannot guarantee it, but we will try everything to get the best results. Did you fill out the laundry slip?

Guest: Yes, I did. When can I have everything back?

Attendant: Your laundry will be delivered by noon tomorrow[2] if you use our regular service.

Guest: That late? Can you deliver it before 5 o'clock this evening? I need to wear the dress to my dinner party!

Attendant: If you are in a hurry, we have express service. You can get your laundry back within two hours, but 50% of the regular charge will be added to your bill. Is that okay?

Guest: I guess I have no choice. I'll use the express service. Charge it to my room, please.

Key & Alternative Expressions

1. This dress needs dry cleaning.
= This blouse should be dry-cleaned.
cf. I'd like to have this suit pressed.
　　Handwash this sweater in cold water, please.
　　Make sure you don't use fabric softener.
　　This knit should be dried on a flat surface.
　　Please remove this chocolate stain from the shirt.

2. Your laundry will be delivered by noon tomorrow.
= Your laundry will be ready by noon tomorrow.
= We can deliver your laundry by noon tomorrow.
= We will return your laundry by noon tomorrow.

B. Handling lost and found items 08-05

Order Taker: Housekeeping Order Taker

Caller	I stayed at your hotel a few days ago, and I believe I left something in my hotel room.
Order Taker	May I have your name and room number, please?
Caller	My name is Dora Brooks, and I don't remember my room number.
Order Taker	That's all right, Ms. Brooks. Do you remember your check-in date?
Caller	Yes. I checked in on November 12.
Order Taker	Could you tell me what you lost, please? And what does it look like?
Caller	It was my necklace. It's made of white gold, and it has a crystal pendant.
Order Taker	Let me check the list, ma'am. May I put you on hold for a moment?
Caller	Sure, go ahead.
	(A few minutes later…)
Order Taker	Hello, Ms. Brooks. You're very lucky! A maid found a necklace in your room, and we are keeping it at Housekeeping. I'm sure this is the one you lost. Do you want me to mail it to the address we have on file?
Caller	Sure. Thank you.
Order Taker	No problem. We'll charge the postage to the credit card you used when you checked out. A receipt and an invoice will be sent to your email.

❖ Say the following sentences in English.
1 체크인 날짜를 기억하십니까?
2 어떻게 생겼습니까?
3 화이트골드로 만들어졌고, 크리스털 펜던트가 달려 있습니다.
4 객실관리부에서 보관하고 있습니다.
5 영수증과 송장은 이메일로 발송될 겁니다.

Essential Expressions | Other Housekeeping Services

1. **Telling guests that a lost item is found**
    A maid found a necklace in your room, and we are keeping it at Housekeeping.
    cf. I'm sorry, but we didn't find anything in your room. I will fill out a lost article report and make sure to contact you if someone finds it.

2. **Asking guests about how they want a lost item back**
    Do you want me to mail it to the address we have on file?
    Do you want it delivered? / Shall I have it delivered? / Do you want me to send it by mail?
    Would you like to pick it up in person or have it delivered?

Exercises

A Choose the best response to each question.

1. When a room needs to be cleaned, which sign should be put out?
   a. "Make up Room" sign
   b. "Do Not Disturb" sign
   c. "Please Reuse Your Towels" sign

2. Who is in charge of fixing things in guest rooms?
   a. a maintenance man
   b. a houseman
   c. a room attendant

3. Which of the following is NOT a responsibility of Housekeeping?
   a. babysitting
   b. guest registration
   c. handling lost & found items

4. Who picks up the guests' laundry?
   a. a room maid
   b. a laundry attendant
   c. an order taker

B Match each sentence with the best reply.

1. May I clean this room now?
2. Is there anything else you need?
3. The heater seems to be broken.
4. When can I have my laundry back?
5. Could you tell me what you lost?

a. I'd like an extra blanket, please.
b. I'm sorry for the inconvenience.
c. Yes, you may. How long will it take?
d. It was my phone charger.
e. It will be delivered by 6 P.M.

C Complete the following conversation with the words in the box.

| housekeeping | laundry | nonallergenic | disturb | make up |

Room Maid: ¹_____. Hello. May I come in?

Guest: Yes, what's the matter?

Room Maid: I'm sorry to ²_____ you, but may I come in to ³_____ your room, ma'am?

Guest: Sure. Come in. Oh, by the way, can you change my pillow to a ⁴_____ foam pillow? And do you have an iron and ironing board? I have some ⁵_____ to iron.

Room Maid: Yes, ma'am. I will set them up in your room right after making up the room.

Role-Playing

A Use the pictures below to practice sending items up to a guest's room. Take turns being a Housekeeping order taker and a guest with your partner.

towel   facial tissue   bathrobe   sewing kit   baby crib

Example

Order Taker   Housekeeping. How may I help you?
Guest   Can you send me a box of facial tissues?
Order Taker   Yes, sir. I will send a box of facial tissues up to your room immediately.

B Use the pictures below to practice handling lost & found items. Take turns being a Housekeeping order taker and a guest with your partner.

watch   cell phone   necklace   earrings   passport

bracelet   wallet   swimsuit   laptop computer   camera

Example

Order Taker   Housekeeping. How may I assist you?
Caller   Yes, I left a pair of earrings in my room last week.
Order Taker   Could you describe them, please?
Caller   They are _____.

Looking into the Hotel Read the following passage that describes what the Housekeeping Department does.

Housekeeping

Housekeeping is one of the departments in the rooms division. The primary duty of Housekeeping is to clean guest rooms, and it provides babysitting and lost and found services as well. The Housekeeping staff members often work as a team to keep every guest's room clean and attractive because the condition of the room has a strong influence on how satisfied the customer is with the hotel. Thus, the Housekeeping Department is often considered vital to a hotel.

There are different positions in Housekeeping: order takers, room attendants, room inspectors, housemen, and laundry staff members are some of them. An order taker takes phone calls from guests' rooms and handles guest requests, complaints, and lost & found items. A room attendant cleans guests' rooms and supplies them with amenities. Once a room attendant finishes her work, a room inspector checks the status of the room in terms of cleanness, facilities, and supplies.

A houseman is mainly in charge of delivering and setting up items guests request for their rooms. He carries heavy linens and towels from the maid carts. A houseman also cleans common areas such as the lobby and a meeting room in a hotel. Laundry staff members provide valet services to guests who need their clothes to be washed, dry-cleaned, or pressed. The majority of a laundry valet's job is to wash the hundreds or thousands of sheets, towels, tablecloths, and napkins that are soiled during the running of a hotel every day. Laundry staff members are also responsible for cleaning the uniforms of the hotel staff members.

Words & Phrases

attractive pleasant to look at
babysitting the act of looking after children while their parents are absent
room inspector an employee who checks that everything in a guest room is in the correct condition
sheet a large piece of cloth that you sleep on or cover yourself with in a bed

soil to make dirty
status condition
supply to give someone something the person wants or needs
valet service a service that helps guests with laundry
vital very important

9
Hotel Facilities

Unit Objectives
◇ At the Business Center
◇ At the Fitness Center

Warming Up

A Look at the picture below. Where in a hotel may you see this? Share your thoughts with your partner.

B Write the correct name for each facility in a hotel.

| gym | sauna | golf driving range | swimming pool |

1 _____ 2 _____ 3 _____ 4 _____

Vocabulary Complete each sentence with the correct word or phrase from the box.

| overseas | copies | rent | fragile | staple | insurance |

1 I have some package I want to send _____.
2 You need bubble wrap when you pack a _____ item.
3 Please make five _____ of this leaflet before our meeting at 2 P.M.
4 You can make sure that your package is safely sent by purchasing shipping _____.
5 Can I _____ a baby crib for my room?
6 Please _____ these pages together.

Hotel Terminology Learn the following words and phrases used in the hotel industry.

business center	a department in a hotel that provides secretarial services, arranges meetings, does typing, sends faxes, prints and photocopies papers, and does other similar work
courier service	a service involving the sending of letters, documents, and parcels directly from one place to another
fitness center	a place where people can enjoy their leisure time by doing exercise, swimming, relaxing, or playing golf
handling charge	the cost of handling (especially the cost of packaging and mailing an order)
invoice	a list of goods or services that someone has bought; a bill

Tips to Know

Video Conferencing System

A video conferencing system is a set of technology that enables people from multiple locations to have a conference without actually meeting in person. The system is mainly designed for online employee training sessions, web seminars, and trans-regional meetings. People can communicate simultaneously by seeing and hearing each other just like they are meeting face to face when they use this system. They can also share data such as documents and media files in real time. Some upscale hotels that are equipped with up-to-date business facilities normally provide video conferencing systems.

Conversation 1: At the Business Center

A. Photocopy service

Agent: Business Center Agent

Agent	Good afternoon, ma'am. How can I help you?
Guest	I would like to copy these documents.
Agent	Certainly, ma'am. How many copies do you need?[1]
Guest	I'd like to make 5 copies of each page, please. Can you staple them as well?
Agent	We can do that, but if you'd like, you can buy presentation binders. They cost 1,000 won each.
Guest	Oh, that would be great. Please put the copies in the binders then.
Agent	Very good, ma'am. Would you like to take a seat for a moment while I make your copies? It will take about 10 minutes.
Guest	Okay. Please take your time. There is no need to hurry.[2]
	(10 minutes later…)
Agent	Your copies are ready, ma'am. Here you are.
Guest	Great. How much do I owe you?[3]
Agent	It is 25,000 won, ma'am.
Guest	Can you charge them to my room account?[4] I'm in room 1615. My name is Stacy Summers.
Agent	Of course, Ms. Summers. Please write your room number and sign this bill.

Key & Alternative Expressions

1. How many copies do you need?
= How many copies should I make?

2. There is no need to hurry.
= I'm not in a hurry. = I don't mind waiting. = There's no rush.
cf. Are you in a hurry (rush), sir?

3. How much do I owe you?
= How much does it cost? = How much will it cost? = How much will that be?

4. Can you charge them to my room account?
= Would you put them on my room account?
= Can you charge them to my room bill, please?
= Charge everything to my room, please.

B. Printing service

09-02

Agent: Business Center Agent

Agent   Good evening. Business center. Diane speaking. How may I assist you?

Guest   Can you print some documents for me? I can't leave my room right now.

Agent   Sure. If you send us the files, we can print them and deliver them to your room.
Our email address is business@sunshine.com.

Guest   That sounds perfect. I will send the files right away.
How long will it take?

Agent   Your copies will be delivered within 20 minutes.
Do you want me to charge the fee to your room account?
Mr. McDonald, you are in room 1815, right?

Guest   Yes, that's right. Please go ahead.

❖ Say the following sentences in English.
1. 이메일로 파일을 보내주시면 저희가 출력해서 객실로 가져다드릴 수 있습니다.
2. 고객님의 출력물은 20분 안에 배달될 겁니다.

C. Courier service

09-03

Agent: Business Center Agent

Guest   Pardon me. I have something I want to send overseas.

Agent   We provide three types of international express mail services: DHL, FedEx, and EMS.
Which service would you like to use?

Guest   What is EMS?

Agent   It is an express mail service provided by the Korean post office.
It takes one or two days longer, but it is cheaper than DHL and FedEx.

Guest   I'm not in a hurry. I will send it by EMS.

Agent   All right. Please fill out this invoice.
Is there anything fragile inside?

Guest   No, there isn't.

Agent   Would you like to purchase insurance for 10 dollars?

Guest   No, thank you.

Agent   There is a handling charge of 10,000 won.
How would you like to pay it?

Guest   Put it on my room bill, please.

❖ Say the following sentences in English.
1. 이 송장을 작성해주십시오.
2. 안에 깨지기 쉬운 물건이 들어 있습니까?
3. 10달러짜리 보험에 가입하시겠습니까?

D. Meeting room service

Agent: Business Center Agent

Agent	Good afternoon, sir. What can I do for you today?
Guest	Hello. Can I reserve a meeting room? There are eight of us.
Agent	When would you like to use the meeting room?
Guest	We need it for the entire day tomorrow starting at 9 A.M.
Agent	We have a room for eight people. The rate is 100,000 won per hour. But if you rent the room for the entire day, you only have to pay for 6 hours.
Guest	We are going to have a presentation there. What services can you provide for us?
Agent	The meeting room has free wireless Internet access and LCD TVs, and we can arrange anything you need for a presentation. You can even rent laptop computers on request.
Guest	Can we order some refreshments in the meeting room?
Agent	Of course, sir. You can order cookies and coffee or tea from room service. You can also preorder them to have them set up in the meeting room at any time you want.
Guest	Excellent! Please arrange 8 personal laptops, and coffee and cookies for eight people then.
Agent	No problem, sir. May I have your name and room number, please?
Guest	I'm Jack Morgan in room 1010.
Agent	You're all set, Mr. Morgan. We will have 8 personal laptops ready and have the kitchen prepare coffee and cookies for eight people. If you'd like to change your reservation, please give us a call.

❖ Say the following sentences in English.
1. 오늘은 무엇을 도와드릴까요?
2. 회의실을 종일 대여하시면, 6시간에 해당하는 비용만 내시면 됩니다.
3. 요청하시면 노트북도 대여하실 수 있습니다.

Essential Expressions — At the Business Center

1. Explaining about service fees
The meeting room rate is 100,000 won per hour.
Presentation binders cost 1,000 won each.
Printing service is free of charge up to 10 pages.
Black and white printing is 1,000 won per page.
Faxing costs vary by length and fax number.

2. Saying that something will be ready
We will have 8 personal laptops ready.
We will have the kitchen prepare coffee and cookies for eight people.
We will arrange a flip chart for you.

Conversation II — At the Fitness Center

A. Gym & Sauna

09-05

Agent: Fitness Center Front Desk Agent

Agent Welcome to the fitness center. How may I assist you?

Guest Good morning. Can I use the fitness center?

Agent Absolutely, ma'am. May I have your room number, please?[1]

Guest I'm staying in room 815. My name is Kelly Miller.

Agent All right, Ms. Miller. We have a gym, indoor and outdoor swimming pools, a golf driving range, and a sauna. Which facility would you like to use today?

Guest I'd like to work out at the gym and use the sauna.

Agent You can use the pool and gym for free, but it costs 30,000 won to use the sauna.

Guest That's okay.
Please charge it to my room account.

Agent Absolutely, ma'am.
May I have your signature on the bill, please?[2]

Guest Sure.

Agent Here is your locker key for the sauna.
The gym is to your left on this floor.[3]
You can access the women's sauna through the gym.

Key & Alternative Expressions

1. **May I have your room number, please?**
   = Could you please tell me your room number?
   = Which room are you staying in?
   = I'll need your room number.

2. **May I have your signature on the bill, please?**
   = Can I get your signature right here, please?
   = Could you sign here, please?
   = Would you sign this, please?

3. **The gym is to your left on this floor.**
   cf. Please go through that door.
   It is behind that door.
   The gym is on the 1st floor.
   Please go up one floor.
   Please go down two floors.

B. Swimming pool 09-06

Agent: Fitness Center Front Desk Agent

Guest   Is there a swimming pool at this hotel?

Agent   Yes, there is. We have both indoor and outdoor swimming pools.

Guest   How can I use them? How much are the entrance fees?

Agent   They are complimentary to hotel guests. All you need to do is tell us your room number. Then, you can get a locker key and change in the locker room.

Guest   That sounds terrific! Are kids allowed in the pools?

Agent   Of course they are. Children can use the outdoor kids' pool. If they want to use the indoor pool, a parent or guardian should be with them.

Guest   I see. What are the opening hours?

Agent   They are open from 6 A.M. to 10 P.M. Just for your information, the outdoor swimming pool is only open from June 15 to August 31.

Guest   I have my swimsuit with me, but I forgot to bring my swim cap. Can I rent one here?

Agent   Certainly, sir. The rental charge for a swim cap is 3,000 won. You can also rent goggles for the same price.

Guest   Thank you for the information. I'll come back with my kids in an hour.

Agent   My pleasure. I will see you then.

❖ Say the following sentences in English.
1. 실내 수영장과 실내 수영장이 모두 있습니다.
2. 저희에게 고객님의 객실 번호만 말씀해주시면 됩니다.
3. 아이들이 실내 수영장을 이용하고 싶어 하면, 부모나 보호자가 동반해야 합니다.

Essential Expressions | At the Fitness Center

1. Telling a guest that a service is free
It is complimentary to hotel guests.
If you are a guest of this hotel, it is complimentary (free).
There is no charge for our hotel guests.

2. Explaining the opening hours of hotel facilities
The pool is open from 6 A.M. to 10 P.M.
The business (opening) hours are from 6 A.M. to 10 P.M.
The operating hours are from 6 A.M. to 10 P.M.
We are open from 6 A.M. to 10 P.M.

3. Responding to "Thank you"
You're welcome. / My pleasure. / No problem. / Any time. / The pleasure is all mine.

Exercises

A Choose the best response to each question.

1. Which service is available for guests to use at the business center?
   a. photocopy service
   b. body composition analysis service
   c. lost & found service

2. Which of the following is NOT likely to be needed for a video conference?
   a. Internet access
   b. an LCD TV
   c. a whiteboard

3. If guests need to send a package overseas, which department in a hotel should they contact?
   a. business center
   b. housekeeping
   c. room service

4. What does the staff need to check before a guest uses the hotel facilities?
   a. the guest's age
   b. the guest's room number
   c. the room rate

B Match each sentence with the best reply.

1. I would like to copy these.
2. They will be ready in about 10 minutes.
3. How long will it take?
4. How large is your party?
5. How much is the entrance fee?

a. Sure. Take your time.
b. How many copies do you need?
c. It is complimentary to hotel guests.
d. There are 10 of us.
e. It will be delivered within 20 minutes.

C Complete the following conversation with the words in the box.

> indoor   fitness center   facility   hours   change

Agent: Welcome to the ¹_____. Which ²_____ would you like to use today?

Guest: Good morning. Can I use the pool?

Agent: Of course, sir. We have both ³_____ and outdoor swimming pools.

Guest: I'd like to visit the outdoor pool. What are the opening ⁴_____?

Agent: It is open from 6 A.M. to 10 P.M.

Guest: Where can I ⁵_____ into my swimsuit?

Agent: You can use the locker room over there.

Role-Playing

A Use the items in the pictures below to practice taking a meeting room reservation. Take turns being a business center agent and a guest with your partner.

LCD TV · wireless Internet · laptop computer · flip chart · whiteboard

office supplies · microphone · table flowers · coffee · water

Example

Agent Do you need anything for your meeting?

Guest Yes. We need _____.

B Use the information below to practice asking and answering questions about the hotel's sports facilities. Take turns being a fitness center front desk agent and a guest.

Fitness Center (3rd Floor)

- **Gym** (6:00 A.M. – 10:00 P.M.)
- **Swimming pools**
  - Indoor pool (7:00 A.M. – 10:00 P.M.)
  - Outdoor pool (10:00 A.M. – 9:00 P.M.)
- **Sauna** (6:00 A.M. – 10:00 P.M.)
- **Golf driving range** (7:00 A.M. – 10:00 P.M.)

Example

Agent Good morning. How may I help you?

Guest What kinds of sports facilities do you have?

Agent We have _____.

Looking into the Hotel — Read the following passage that describes what guests can do in the business center and fitness center.

Business Center & Fitness Center

A business center at a hotel is a place that offers guests various services and equipment to help them do office work. For example, the staff members at a business center do printing, copying, photocopying, typing, faxing, and document binding for guests. In addition, secretarial services, translation and interpretation services, and courier services are available.

A business center is also usually fully equipped for business meetings and conferences. Guests can enjoy high-speed Internet connections and rent equipment such as laptop computers, beam projectors, LCD screens, flip charts, and whiteboards if they need them for their meetings. Facilities for video conferencing can be set up as well. Even office supplies such as paper clips, papers, and binders are available for purchase.

A fitness center at a hotel is a place where guests can enjoy their leisure time doing exercise, swimming, relaxing in the sauna, or playing golf. Guests can also get their body composition analyzed and measure their blood pressure or body fat.

Words & Phrases

analyze to examine something closely
bind to tie or fasten things together
body composition the proportion of fat, muscle, and bone of a human body, which can be used to determine one's physical health
courier a person who takes letters or parcels from one place to another
equipment tools or supplies

exercise the act of working out
flip chart a board with large sheets of paper which can be turned over, usually used in a meeting
interpretation translation; an explanation of what something means
measure to find the exact size or amount of something
office supplies materials regularly used in offices

10
Room Service

Unit Objectives
◇ Taking Orders for Room Service
◇ Delivering Room Service

Warming Up

A Look at the picture below. Who is the man? What is he doing? Share your thoughts with your partner.

B Write the correct name for each egg dish.

scrambled eggs   fried egg (sunny side up)   omelet   boiled egg   poached egg

1 _____   2 _____   3 _____   4 _____   5 _____

Vocabulary
Complete each sentence with the correct word or phrase from the box.

> meal   repeat   rare   take   boiled   on the way

1. May I _____ your order?
2. Please wait a few minutes. Your order is _____.
3. Enjoy your _____.
4. How do you like your eggs, fried or _____?
5. I ordered my steak well done, but this seems too _____ to me.
6. May I _____ your order back to you?

Hotel Terminology
Learn the following words and phrases used in the hotel industry.

doorknob service	a type of service for ordering breakfast (Guests hang doorknob menus on the door handles, and then waiters collect them during the night shift.)
order slip	an order pad
order taker	an employee who takes a guest's order
over easy	(of a fried egg) fried on both sides for a short time (Fried eggs can be cook in a variety of ways: over easy, over medium, over hard, over well.)
room service	a service in which food and drinks are served in a guest's room; the people who do this work
service cart	a small table with wheels used for serving food and drinks in a guest's room, usually with food warming racks

Tips to Know

Continental Breakfast vs. American Breakfast

Continental Breakfast
- **breads:** toasted bread, English muffins, bagels, biscuits, croissant, danish pastry
- **beverages:** coffee, tea, orange juice

American Breakfast
- **breads:** toasted bread, English muffins, bagels, biscuits, croissant, danish pastry
- **beverages:** coffee, tea, orange juice
- **hot main dishes**
  eggs: fried eggs, scrambled eggs, boiled eggs, poached eggs, omelets
  meats: ham, bacon, sausage
  potatoes: hash browns, home fries

Conversation 1: Taking Orders for Room Service

A. Taking a room service order

Order Taker: Room Service Order Taker

Order Taker	Good evening. Room service. Alex speaking. How may I assist you?
Guest	Hi. I'm Theresa Perry in room 1920. How can I order breakfast for tomorrow?
Order Taker	I can take your order on the phone now, or you can fill out a breakfast order card and hang it on the doorknob.
Guest	I'd like to order on the phone now.
Order Taker	Sure. What would you like to order, Ms. Perry?
Guest	I'd like to have the American breakfast, please.
Order Taker	All right, ma'am. How would you like your eggs?
Guest	I'd like an omelet with no cheese, please.[1]
Order Taker	What kind of juice would you like, ma'am?
Guest	Apple juice, and I'd like some morning pastries and a cappuccino, please.
Order Taker	What time would you like your breakfast tomorrow?[2]
Guest	Can I have it at 7:00 tomorrow morning?
Order Taker	Absolutely, ma'am. We will deliver it to your room by 7:00 A.M. tomorrow. Do you need anything else, Ms. Perry?
Guest	That's all.
Order Taker	Let me repeat your order. You ordered the American breakfast with an omelet with no cheese, apple juice, morning pastries, and a cappuccino at 7:00 tomorrow morning. Is it correct?
Guest	Yes, you bet!
Order Taker	Thank you for calling room service. Have a good night.

Key & Alternative Expressions

1. I'd like an omelet with no cheese, please.
   cf. I want a hamburger with no onions.
   Let me have some French fries with extra ketchup.

2. What time would you like your breakfast tomorrow?
   = When would you like to have your breakfast tomorrow?
   = What time should we deliver your breakfast tomorrow?
   = What time would you like your breakfast to be delivered (ready)?
   = What time would you like to be served tomorrow?
   = Do you want us to deliver it right away or at a specific time?

B. Taking an order for breakfast

Order Taker: Room Service Order Taker

Order Taker	Good morning. Room service. Sharon speaking. How may I help you?
Guest	Good morning. I am in room 1004. I'd like to order the continental breakfast for two, please.
Order Taker	What kind of juice would you like, sir?
Guest	One orange juice and one grapefruit juice with a croissant, please.
Order Taker	I'm terribly sorry, but we are out of grapefruit juice. Instead of grapefruit juice, would you like to try our strawberry juice? Strawberries are in season now.
Guest	Oh, that sounds great!
Order Taker	Thank you, Mr. Wood. Do you want coffee or tea?
Guest	Coffee, please. That will be all.
Order Taker	Thank you. It will take about 15 minutes.

❖ Say the following sentences in English.
1 어떤 주스를 드시겠습니까?
2 딸기가 요즘 제철입니다.

C. Taking an order for lunch

Order Taker: Room Service Order Taker

Order Taker	Good afternoon. Room service. This is Miranda. How can I help you?
Guest	Hi, Miranda. This is Henry Moyer in room 1212. I'd like to order some room service, please. What is today's soup?
Order Taker	It's a tomato-based Manhattan clam chowder, sir.
Guest	Then let me have two bowls of today's soup, a club sandwich, and a cheeseburger, please.
Order Taker	How would you like your burger cooked?
Guest	Medium well done, please. Does it come with French fries?
Order Taker	Yes, it does. Do you need anything to drink?
Guest	Yes, two colas and extra ketchup on the side, please.
Order Taker	I see. Your order will be delivered within 20 minutes.

❖ Say the following sentences in English.
1 버거는 얼마나 익혀드릴까요?
2 감자튀김이 같이 나오나요?
3 케첩은 양을 많이 해서 따로 주세요.

D. Taking an order for dinner

Order Taker: Room Service Order Taker

Order Taker	Good evening. Room service. Chris speaking. How may I help you?
Guest	Good evening. I would like to order dinner, please.
Order Taker	Certainly. May I have your room number, please?
Guest	It is room 630.
Order Taker	All right, Ms. Brooks. May I take your order now?
Guest	Yes. I would like to have the beef tenderloin and a glass of red wine, please.
Order Taker	How would you like your steak, ma'am?
Guest	Medium rare, please.
Order Taker	Would you like some soup or salad?
Guest	One Caesar salad, please.
Order Taker	What would you like for dessert?
Guest	Mango pudding and green tea, please.
Order Taker	Okay. Is there anything else, Ms. Brooks?
Guest	No, thank you. How long will it take?
Order Taker	I am afraid it will take more than 25 minutes since we have a lot of orders right now.
Guest	That's all right.

❖ **Say the following sentences in English.**
1. 수프나 샐러드 하시겠습니까?
2. 디저트는 무엇으로 드릴까요?
3. 죄송하지만 현재 주문량이 많아서 25분 이상 걸릴 겁니다.

Essential Expressions | **Taking Orders for Room Service**

1. Taking an order
What would you like to order?
What would you like to have for dinner?

2. Asking how a guest would like a steak
How would you like your steak?
How do you like your steak done (cooked)?

3. Telling a guest when room service will be delivered
It will take **about** 10 minutes.
Your order will be delivered **within** 10 minutes.
The server will be up **in** a few minutes.
We will send them up **in** about 15 minutes.
Your order will be there **in** about 20 minutes.
It will take **more than** 25 minutes because we have a lot of orders right now.

Conversation II  Delivering Room Service

A. Checking on an order & delivering room service   10-05

Order Taker: Room Service Order Taker / **Waiter:** Room Service Waiter

Order Taker	Good morning. Room service. This is Paul. May I help you?
Guest	I ordered my breakfast to arrive at 7:00 yesterday, but can I add one more breakfast like I ordered yesterday?
Order Taker	Are you Ms. Perry in room 1920?
Guest	Yes, that's me.
Order Taker	Please hold the line for a second. I'll check with the kitchen.
	(A few seconds later…)
Order Taker	Thank you for waiting. Your order is on the way.[1] Your new order will take about 10 more minutes.[2] Is that okay with you?
Guest	Excellent! Thank you.
Order Taker	You're welcome, Ms. Perry.
Waiter	Room service!
Guest	Come on in, please.[3]
Waiter	Good morning, Ms. Perry. I brought your breakfast. Where would you like to eat?
Guest	Please put everything on this table.
Waiter	All right, ma'am. Here you are. I will be back with your second order in a moment.
Guest	Thank you.
Waiter	My pleasure, Ms. Perry. Enjoy your meal.

Key & Alternative Expressions

1. Your order is on the way.
= It will be there soon. = Your order will be up shortly.

2. Your new order will take about 10 more minutes.
= We can deliver your order in about 10 minutes.
= I will be back with your order in about 10 minutes.

3. Come on in, please.
= Please come in. The door isn't locked.
cf. One moment. I'm coming.

B. Handling mistakes

Waiter: Room Service Waiter

Waiter	Room service! May I come in?
Guest	Please do.
Waiter	Good afternoon, Ms. Terry. I brought the lunch you ordered.
Guest	Thank you. Could you set up a table over there, please?
Waiter	Certainly. Here you are.
Guest	Very good.
Waiter	Is there anything else you need, ma'am?
Guest	Well… I don't see my drinks. I ordered two colas.
Waiter	Oh, let me check your order slip… I'm really sorry, ma'am. The order taker must have made a mistake. I'll get your drinks immediately.
	(A few minutes later…)
Waiter	I brought your drinks, Ms. Terry. Here you are. And may I have your signature here, please?
Guest	That was fast! Sure.
Waiter	Thank you. And I apologize for the inconvenience again. I will be back to pick up the service cart in an hour. Enjoy your meal, Ms. Terry.

❖ Say the following sentences in English.
1. 저쪽에 테이블을 설치해 주시겠어요?
2. 주문서를 확인해보겠습니다.
3. 한 시간 뒤에 서비스카트를 찾으러 오겠습니다.

Essential Expressions | Delivering Room Service

1. Acknowledging mistakes
The order taker must have made a mistake.
I'm afraid there must have been a mistake.
That is our mistake (fault).
We made an error with your order.

2. Saying that you will get something for a guest
I'll get your drinks immediately.
I'll be right back with your drinks.
I will bring your drinks right away.

3. Hoping a guest enjoys a meal
Enjoy your meal (breakfast/lunch/dinner/drink)!
Enjoy it! / Please enjoy. / Bon appetite!

Exercises

A Choose the best response to each question.

1. Which items CANNOT be ordered from room service?
   a. an appetizer
   b. an alcoholic beverage
   c. a sewing kit

2. Which is NOT a type of fried egg?
   a. sunny side up
   b. poached
   c. over easy

3. What breakfast includes egg dishes?
   a. American breakfast
   b. continental breakfast
   c. both of them

4. Who is responsible for collecting food trays from guest rooms?
   a. an order taker
   b. a room service waiter
   c. a room maid

B Match each sentence with the best reply.

1. I'd like to have some breakfast.
2. How would you like your eggs?
3. What time should we deliver your breakfast tomorrow?
4. How would you like your burger?
5. Would you sign here, please?

a. I'd like scrambled eggs, please.
b. Can I have it by 7:00 tomorrow morning?
c. What would you like to order, sir?
d. Sure. Here it is.
e. Well-done, please.

C Complete the following conversation with the words in the box.

| out of | come with | in season | bowl | medium rare |

Order Taker: What would you like to order?

Guest: I'd like to order a ¹_____ of broccoli soup, the sirloin steak, and a glass of red wine, please. Does the steak ²_____ any vegetables?

Order Taker: Yes, it does. How would you like your steak?

Guest: ³_____, please. I also want to have a glass of guava juice.

Order Taker: I'm sorry, but we are ⁴_____ guava juice now. Why don't you try our tangerine juice? Tangerines are ⁵_____ now.

Unit 10 | 119

Role-Playing

Use the room service menu below to practice taking an order from a guest. Take turns being a room service order taker and a guest with your partner.

🛎 Room Service Menu 🛎

BREAKFAST

CONTINENTAL BREAKFAST ₩29,000
Choice of Freshly Squeezed Orange, Grapefruit, Tomato, or Apple Juice
Basket of Morning Pastries or Toast
Freshly Brewed Coffee or Tea

AMERICAN BREAKFAST ₩36,000
Choice of Freshly Squeezed Orange, Grapefruit, Tomato, or Apple Juice
Two Eggs Prepared Any Style with Bacon, Ham, or Sausage
Basket of Morning Pastries or Toast
Freshly Brewed Coffee or Tea

EGGS AND SPECIALTIES
Two Eggs Prepared Any Style with Bacon, Ham, or Sausage	₩16,000
White Omelet with Tomatoes, Asparagus, and Mushrooms	₩18,000
Freshly Baked Waffle with Strawberries and Whipped Cream	₩16,000
Buttermilk Pancakes Topped with Walnuts and Apricot Sauce	₩16,000
French Toast with Fresh Fruits and Maple Syrup	₩15,000
Fresh Fruits	₩22,000

BEVERAGES

FRESHLY SQUEEZED JUICE ₩12,000
Orange, Grapefruit, Tomato, Apple, Kiwi Juice

SOFT DRINKS ₩12,000
Cola, Diet Cola, Ginger Ale

TEA ₩12,000
Darjeeling, English Breakfast, Ceylon, Jasmine, Chamomile, Green Tea

COFFEE
Americano, Espresso	₩11,000
Café Latte, Cappuccino	₩12,000

Example

Order Taker: Good morning. Room service. How may I help you?
Guest: I would like to order some breakfast, please.
Order Taker: _____.

Looking into the Hotel Read the following passage that describes room service.

10-07

Room Service

One of the exclusive services that high-end upscale hotels and resorts provide is room service. Room service, or in-room dining, is a hotel service that enables guests to have their meals and drinks delivered to their rooms.

Room service is also one of the subdivisions of the Food & Beverage Department at hotel and resort properties. It usually operates on a 24-hour basis and mainly consists of three types of staff members. They are order takers, waiters, and cooks.

Order takers take guests' orders and pass them to the cooks in the kitchen. Order takers are also responsible for handling guests' complaints. Waiters deliver guests' orders to their room, set dishes up in requested places, and collect trays and carts. Waiters also take doorknob menu cards from doors during the night shift and send the guests' orders to the kitchen. Cooks prepare the food exactly the way the guests want. They often prepare food that is not on the menu for guests as long as all the ingredients are available.

Words & Phrases

collect to go and get something from the place where it is left
cook a person whose job is to prepare food
doorknob a round handle on a door
enable make someone able to do something

high-end of high quality; very expensive
ingredient a food that you use to make a particular dish
property a thing or building owned by someone
subdivision a part of something which is itself a part of something larger

11

Restaurants & Bars

Unit Objectives

◇ Reserving Tables & Greeting Customers
◇ Taking Orders & Handling Payments

Warming Up

A Look at the picture below. Where in a hotel is it? What kinds of activities can take place here? Share your thoughts with your partner.

B Write the correct job title for each hotel staff member.

waiter/waitress   greeter   busboy   bartender

1 _____ 2 _____ 3 _____ 4 _____

Vocabulary
Match each word or phrase with the correct picture.

| 1 T-bone steak ____ | 2 sirloin steak ____ | 3 Caesar salad ____ | 4 fried fish ____ |
| 5 sorbet ____ | 6 club sandwich ____ | 7 rye bread ____ | 8 silverware ____ |

a. (rye bread) b. (Caesar salad) c. (sorbet) d. (club sandwich)
e. (sirloin steak) f. (T-bone steak) g. (fried fish) h. (silverware)

Hotel Terminology
Learn the following words and phrases used in the hotel industry.

à la carte menu	a menu with a separate price for each dish (↔ table d'hôte)
aperitif	an alcoholic drink that you have before a meal
busboy	an employee who takes dirty dishes away from tables
entrée	the main course at restaurants or formal dinners
greeter	an employee who welcomes customers politely in a restaurant
hors d'oeuvre	small amounts of food that are served before the main part of a meal; an appetizer
table d'hôte	a complete meal consisting of a number of courses served at a fixed price with a limited choice of dishes (courses: appetizer, soup, fish, entrée, salad, dessert, and beverage)
waiter/waitress	an employee who serves food and drinks to diners in a restaurant

Tips to Know

Dinner Table Etiquette at Hotel Restaurants – 5 Don'ts

1. Don't wear strong perfume. The heavy scent of it may prevent other people from enjoying the delicate aromas and flavors of their food and beverages.
2. Don't put personal belongings such as cell phones, keys, wallets, and purses on the table.
3. Don't yell or wave to get a waiter's attention. Instead, try to make eye contact with the waiter or raise your hand to call him.
4. Don't pick up a fallen piece of silverware. Just signal a waiter quietly to replace it with a new one.
5. Don't wipe your face or neck with your napkin or tuck your napkin under your chin.

Conversation 1: Reserving Tables & Greeting Customers

A. Taking a reservation   11-01

Greeter	Good afternoon. Grace Restaurant. Ashley speaking. How may I help you?
Customer	Hello. I would like to reserve a table.[1]
Greeter	Certainly, sir. When would you like to dine here?
Customer	Tomorrow evening at seven.
Greeter	How many people are there in your party?
Customer	There will be two of us.
Greeter	What name should I make the reservation under?
Customer	Under the name of Logan Iverson.[2]
Greeter	Could you spell your last name, please?
Customer	Yes. It's I-V-E-R-S-O-N.
Greeter	All right. Can I have your contact number, please?
Customer	Sure. My number is 070-1078-7880
Greeter	So that's a table for 2 tomorrow night at seven for Mr. Iverson. Is that correct?[3]
Customer	That's right.
Greeter	Thank you for calling, Mr. Iverson. We look forward to seeing you tomorrow.

Key & Alternative Expressions

1. I would like to reserve a table.
= I would like to make a dinner reservation.
= I'd like to book a table for two.
= Could I reserve a table (in the corner / by the window / in the nonsmoking area)?
= I need to make a reservation (for tomorrow evening).

2. Under the name of Logan Iverson.
= I made a reservation for (in the name of / under the name of) Logan Iverson.

3. So that's a table for 2 tomorrow night at seven for Mr. Iverson. Is that correct?
= This is a reservation for 2 tomorrow at 7 P.M. Is that correct?
= A table for 2 tomorrow night at seven in the name of Mr. Iverson. Is that right?
= I have reserved a table for 2 tomorrow night at seven for you. Would you like something else?
cf. May I repeat your reservation?
   Let me repeat your reservation details.

B. Assigning a table for customers with a reservation

Greeter	Good evening, sir. Welcome to the Universe. Do you have a reservation?
Customer	Yes, I have.
Greeter	Under what name is it, sir?
Customer	Todd Collins. I reserved a table for two.
Greeter	All right, Mr. Collins. Where would you prefer to sit?
Customer	We want a table in a quiet corner. We are having an important business meeting.
Greeter	Very well, sir. We have one in the corner. I will show you to your table. Would you come this way, please?
Customer	Thank you.
Greeter	How do you like this table?
Customer	It's great.
Greeter	Please take a seat. Here are your menus. Your waiter will be with you in a moment.

❖ Say the following sentences in English.
1 어떤 분 성함으로 예약하셨습니까?
2 선호하시는 좌석이 있습니까?
3 구석에 자리가 하나 있습니다. 제가 테이블로 안내해드리겠습니다.
4 이쪽으로 오시겠습니까?
5 이 테이블 어떠십니까?

C. Assigning a table for walk-in customers

Greeter	Good morning. Do you have a reservation?
Customer	No, we don't.
Greeter	I'm afraid all our tables are taken. Would you mind waiting until one is free?
Customer	How long will that take?
Greeter	I am not a hundred percent sure, but I believe it will take about 10 minutes.
Customer	That's all right. We can wait.
Greeter	If you don't mind sitting separately, we can seat you very soon.
Customer	Oh, no. We want to have a table together.
Greeter	All right. Could you take a seat over there? I'll call you when a table is ready.
	(A few minutes later…)
Greeter	I'm very sorry to have kept you waiting. We have a table for you now. This way, please.

❖ **Say the following sentences in English.**
1 죄송하지만 테이블이 다 찼습니다.
2 빈 테이블이 날 때까지 기다리셔야 하는데 괜찮으십니까?
3 저쪽 자리에 앉아주시겠습니까?
4 빈 테이블이 나면 불러드리겠습니다.
5 기다리게 해드려서 대단히 죄송합니다.

D. At the Bar

Bartender	How are you this evening?
Customer 1	Fine, thanks.
Bartender	Would you care for something to drink?
Customer 1	Sure. I will have a shot of bourbon, please.
Bartender	Would you like that straight up or on the rocks?
Customer 1	Make it a double shot on the rocks, please.
Bartender	What can I get you, ma'am?
Customer 2	Can you recommend a cocktail that isn't too sweet?
Bartender	Well, let me see… I would recommend a gin and tonic if you prefer a cocktail that isn't sweet.
Customer 2	Okay. Give me a gin and tonic with a lime in it, please.
Bartender	Certainly, ma'am.

❖ Say the following sentences in English.
1 마실 것 좀 드릴까요?
2 스트레이트로 드릴까요, 온더록스로 드릴까요?
3 달지 않은 칵테일을 찾으시면 진토닉을 추천해드리겠습니다.

Essential Expressions · Reserving Tables & Greeting Customers

1. Asking guests if they like the table
How do you like this table?
What do you think of this table?
Will this table be fine?
Would you like this table?

2. Telling customers they have to wait
I'm afraid all our tables are taken. Would you mind waiting until one is free?
Unfortunately, we don't have any tables available at the moment. Would you mind waiting until one becomes available?
We're full at the moment. Would you mind waiting for a while?
Could you take a seat over there? I'll call you when a table is ready.

3. Suggesting an order for alcoholic beverages
Would you care for something to drink?
What can I get you (to drink)?
Can I get you something to drink?
What would you like to drink?

Conversation 11: Taking Orders & Handling Payments

A. Taking orders

Waiter	Good evening, ladies. Welcome to the Rose Restaurant. My name is Ryan. I'll be serving you this evening. Would you care for an aperitif before your meal?[1]
Customer 1	Yes, I'll have a glass of sherry, please.
Customer 2	Make that two, please.
Waiter	Yes, ma'am. Two glasses of sherry. Have you decided what to order?
Customer 1	No, we haven't decided yet.
Waiter	Take your time. I'll be back to take your orders with your drinks.
	(Later, the waiter comes back with the drinks.)
Waiter	Here are your drinks. May I take your order now?
Customer 1	Yes. I'd like the sirloin steak and the garden salad with Italian dressing.
Waiter	Sure. How would you like your steak?
Customer 1	Medium, please.
Waiter	All right. And you, ma'am?
Customer 2	I want to try something special from the à la carte menu. What would you recommend?
Waiter	Why don't you try our fried fish topped with crispy garlic chips, ma'am?[2] It is served with hand-cut fries and mixed salad. It's also today's special.
Customer 2	That sounds great. I'll have that. I'd like French dressing for my salad, please.
Waiter	Certainly. The fried fish and French dressing on a mixed salad. Would you like anything else, ma'am?
Customer 2	No, thank you.
Waiter	Very good. I'll be back with your dishes.

Key & Alternative Expressions

1. Would you care for an aperitif before your meal?
   = Would you like a drink to start?
   = Can I get you something to drink before your meal?

2. Why don't you try our fried fish topped with crispy garlic chips, ma'am?
   = I'd recommend the fried fish.
   = How about the fried fish?
   = Have you tried the fried fish? You really should try it.

B. Checking on diners

11-06

Waitress	Here you are. Enjoy your meal.
	(A few minutes later...)
Waitress	How is everything?
Customer	It's really good!
	Could we have a little more bread, please?
Waitress	Certainly. Is there anything else?
	Would you like another glass of wine?
Customer	That would be great. Could we have another round?
Waitress	Of course. I'll be right back with your bread and wine.

❖ Say the following sentences in English.
1 식사 맛있게 하십시오.
2 식사는 어떠십니까?
3 와인 한 잔 더 하시겠습니까?
4 저희 한 잔씩 더 주시겠어요?

C. Suggesting desserts

11-07

Waitress	I'm sorry to interrupt. May I take your plates?
Customer 1	Yes. We're finished.
Waitress	Did you enjoy your meal?
Customer 2	Everything was excellent.
	I especially enjoyed the sea bass.
Waitress	I'm glad you liked the food.
	Would you like some dessert?
Customer 1	Yes, please. Let me have the lemon sorbet and decaffeinated coffee, please.
Customer 2	I will have a slice of cheesecake and a cappuccino, please.
Waitress	Certainly. I will serve your desserts shortly.

❖ Say the following sentences in English.
1 실례합니다.
2 접시를 치워도 되겠습니까?
3 식사는 입에 맞으셨습니까?
4 맛있게 드셨다니 다행입니다.
5 후식 좀 드시겠습니까?

D. Handling payments　　11-08

Customer 1	Could we have the check, please? We would like to split the bill.
Waiter	No problem, ma'am. I'll bring separate checks. Just a moment, please.
	(A few minutes later...)
Waiter	Ladies, here are your checks.
Customer 1	Is the service charge included?
Waiter	Yes. A 10% service charge is included in the bill.
Customer 1	Can we pay here at the table?
Waiter	Of course. How will you be paying?
Customer 1	I'm going to pay with cash, and she is going to charge it to her room.
Waiter	All right, ma'am.
Customer 1	Here you are. Keep the change.
Waiter	Thank you. *(To customer 2)* Can I have your signature and room number here, please?
Customer 2	Sure. Here you are.
Waiter	It was my pleasure to serve you today. We look forward to seeing you again soon.

❖ **Say the following sentences in English.**
1 계산을 따로 하고 싶은데요.
2 봉사료 10%가 계산서에 포함되어 있습니다.
3 여기에 고객님 서명과 객실 번호를 받을 수 있을까요?

Essential Expressions　Taking Orders and Handling Payments

1. **Taking an order**
   Have you decided what to order? / May I take your order now? / Are you ready to order?
   What would you like to order? / What would you like to have (for dinner)?

2. **Offering to clean off the table**
   May I take your plates (away)? / May I clear away the dishes? / May I clean the table?

3. **Asking about meals**
   Did you enjoy your meal? / How was everything? / How did you like your meal?

4. **Suggesting desserts**
   Would you like some dessert? / Would you like to see the dessert menu?

5. **Saying goodbye to diners**
   It was my pleasure to serve you today. We look forward to seeing you again (soon).
   Thank you for dining with us. I hope you enjoyed your meal. Please come again.
   Have a nice day (evening). We hope to see you again.

Exercises

A Choose the best response to each question.

1. What do you call a type of drink that customers have before their meals?
   a. appetizer
   b. aperitif
   c. hors d'oeuvres

2. What do you call a menu that customers can choose dishes with separate prices from?
   a. à la carte menu
   b. table d'hôte
   c. hors d'oeuvre

3. Who takes away dishes?
   a. a busboy
   b. a greeter
   c. a restaurant manager

4. Which is an appropriate way to call a waiter?
   a. To make eye contact with the waiter
   b. To wave at the waiter enthusiastically
   c. To yell at the waiter

B Match each sentence with the best reply.

1. Can I reserve a table for two?
2. How do you like this table?
3. Would you care for something to drink?
4. What do you recommend?
5. How would you like your check?

a. Make it separate, please.
b. Sure, I will have a whiskey on the rocks, please.
c. Why don't you try the sirloin steak?
d. It's fine.
e. Certainly, sir. For what day will that be?

C Complete the following conversation with the words in the box.

> dine   taken   seat   mind   show

Greeter Good morning. Welcome to the Marina.

Customer Can we ¹_____ here now? We don't have a reservation.

Greeter I'm afraid all our tables are ²_____. Do you ³_____ waiting for 10 minutes? I will ⁴_____ you as soon as a table is ready.

Customer I'm very sorry to have kept you waiting. We have a table for you now. I will ⁵_____ you to the table.

Role-Playing

Practice taking orders by using the following à la carte menu. Take turns being a waiter/waitress and a customer with your partner.

✕ Menu ✕

APPETIZERS & SOUPS

Caesar Salad	₩21,000
Chicken Salad	₩25,000
Mushroom Cream Soup	₩20,000
Seafood Soup with Garlic Toast	₩21,000

PASTAS & SANDWICHES

Seafood Spaghetti with Tomato Sauce or Cream Sauce	₩29,000
Bolognese Spaghetti	₩27,000
Hamburger	₩29,000
Cheeseburger (Choice of Cheddar, Gruyere, or Brie Cheese)	₩33,000
Club Sandwich	₩27,000

GRILL

Beef Tenderloin	₩49,000
Ribeye	₩53,000

DESSERTS

Mango Pudding	₩14,000
Ice Cream (Vanilla, Strawberry, Chocolate)	₩12,000
Sherbet (Mango, Raspberry, Yoghurt)	₩12,000

BEVERAGES

FRESHLY SQUEEZED JUICE

Orange, Grapefruit, Tomato, Apple, Kiwi	₩12,000

SOFT DRINKS

Cola, Diet Cola, Sprite	₩12,000

TEA

Darjeeling, English Breakfast, Ceylon, Jasmine, Chamomile, Green Tea	₩12,000

COFFEE

Americano, Espresso	₩11,000
Café Latte, Cappuccino	₩12,000

Example

Waiter   Good afternoon, sir. May I take your order?
Customer   I would like a hamburger, please.
Waiter   _____.

Looking into the Hotel Read the following passage that explains about hotel restaurants.

Restaurants

Most full service hotels & resorts have several fine dining restaurants. Fine dining restaurants offer special services with specific dedicated meal courses. The interiors of these restaurants are of high quality, and they are also very spacious. The wait staff is highly trained and often wears formal attire. These hotel restaurants have certain dining rules that people are generally expected to follow, often including a dress code.

There are three main reasons why diners choose to eat at a hotel restaurant despite its very expensive prices: the atmosphere, service, and menu. Hotel restaurants try their best to keep their atmosphere relaxing and pleasant by taking many factors into consideration, such as the layout of the tables, the lighting, and the music. They try to put enough space between each table to allow customers to have some privacy. The restaurants don't make the lights too bright for diners. They keep the volume of the music low in order not to disturb customers. Some hotel restaurants even decide not to have any music at all for fear that it will overpower the dining space.

The wait staff is as important as the elements above. The service that the wait staff provides goes far beyond taking orders from customers and delivering food to tables. Waiters look for signals from customers, anticipate what kind of service individuals want, and then give personalized service to each customer. Waiters also need to have professional knowledge about all the food served. They should be able to answer all questions customers have about the menu or wine. They should also be ready to make menu recommendations if asked.

Words & Phrases

atmosphere the mood or feeling that a place has; ambience
attire the clothes a person is wearing
dedicated devoted; wholehearted
diner someone who is eating a meal in a restaurant
dress code a set of rules about what people should wear in a particular place
layout the way that something is arranged
lighting equipment for producing light
overpower to spoil something by having much stronger power
personalized designed to be suitable for a particular person
take into consideration to think about a particular thing when making a decision

Unit Objectives

◇ Guest Complaints
◇ Guest Problems

12 Complaints & Problems

Warming Up

A Look at the picture below. What seems to be the problem? Share your thoughts with your partner.

B What should hotel staff members say to guests with complaints? Check the correct boxes.

a. I'm very sorry for the inconvenience. ☐	b. Please accept my apology. ☐
c. I've been working hard. ☐	d. Please give me a gratuity for my sincere service. ☐
e. This is someone else's fault. ☐	f. Please forgive us for the mistake. ☐
g. I'm very sorry. Could you tell me what exactly happened, please? ☐	h. I'm terribly sorry, but these things happen. ☐

Vocabulary
Match each word or phrase with its correct definition.

1. report
2. upgrade
3. manager
4. deduct
5. replace
6. spill
7. overcook
8. relief
9. flush
10. clog

a. to take off; to remove
b. to give someone a better room in a hotel
c. to accidentally let a liquid flow out of its container
d. to tell someone that something has happened
e. a feeling of comfort that someone gets when something unpleasant has not happen
f. to give someone a new one
g. to make water go through a toilet by pressing a handle
h. to cook food for too long
i. an employee who is in charge of a department
j. to block something so that nothing can pass through

Hotel Terminology
Learn the following words and phrases used in the hotel industry.

chef	a professional cook who works in a hotel, especially the main cook
complimentary	free; courtesy; on the house
safety deposit box	a strong metal box with a lock in which people can keep their money or valuable things, usually located in a guest room or at the front desk in a hotel
welcome card	a paper card that is put in guest rooms to convey a message that a hotel welcomes their guests

Tips to Know

Employee Empowerment

Employee empowerment means giving frontline employees more freedom, flexibility, and power to make decisions on the spot without asking their superiors. In the hotel industry, employee empowerment is especially important because it provides some practical advantages to a hotel. First, customer satisfaction will increase since empowered workers can respond to guests' problems and complaints more quickly and flexibly. Second, employee satisfaction will also improve. Studies show that empowered staff members tend to feel more motivated and involved in their work. The reason is that they take personal pride in providing guests with high-quality services on their own, thus contributing to their company.

Conversation 1: Guest Complaints

A. Complaints about room facilities   12-01

Manager: Front Desk Manager

Receptionist	Good evening. Front desk. Ted speaking. How may I help you?
Guest	I just checked into room 707, but there is a problem with it.
Receptionist	What exactly is the problem?
Guest	There's no hot water coming out.[1]
Receptionist	I'm sorry, Ms. Murphy. I'll send someone up immediately.
	(1 hour later…)
Guest	Hello. May I speak to Ted?
Receptionist	Speaking. How can I help you?
Guest	I asked you to send someone up about an hour ago, but no one has showed up yet. It's been a long day, and I desperately need a hot shower. I really need you to do something about it right now.
Receptionist	I'm terribly sorry for the inconvenience, Ms. Murphy. I will have the repairman rush there now.
Guest	No, no. I can't just sit here and wait another hour for someone to appear. I want you to change my room.
Receptionist	I'm sorry, but we have a full house today, ma'am. There is nothing I can do about it.
Guest	Can I speak to the manager?
Receptionist	Sure. One moment, please.
Manager	This is the front desk manager, Dewey Carson. I heard you are not happy with our service. I sincerely apologize for the unpleasant experience you just had.
Guest	I never expected such bad service at your hotel. The room has a couple of major issues, and your receptionist was being so stiff and totally lacks flexibility. I'm really disappointed.
Manager	I understand, ma'am.[2] Again, I'm very sorry for the oversight. I've upgraded your room to a suite. I'll send up a bellman with a new key right away. I assure you that it won't happen again.[3]

Key & Alternative Expressions

1. There is no hot water coming out.
   cf. The safety deposit box is not working.
       The TV is broken.
       The light bulb has burned out.
       The electric kettle won't turn on.
       The alarm clock radio is malfunctioning.
       Something has gone wrong with the hair dryer.

2. I understand, ma'am.
   = I can imagine how frustrating it must have been.
   = I realize this matter is very important to you.
   = I know the incident must have been very unpleasant for you.

3. I assure you that it won't happen again.
   = I will make sure this won't happen again.
   = We will take steps to ensure this will never happen again.
   = I give you my word this won't happen again.
   = You have my word this will not happen again.
   = Please rest assured that such a thing will not happen again.

B. Complaints about mischarges

Cashier — Here is your bill. Please check it over to see if there is anything wrong, Mr. White.

Guest — This isn't right. There is a minibar charge here, but I didn't use it at all.

Cashier — Let me check on the detailed bill, sir. You were charged for five cans of soft drinks.

Guest — I just took them out of the fridge to make room for my mineral water.

Cashier — Now I see. The minibar staff member probably thought you drank them all. I'm sorry for the inconvenience. I will deduct them from your bill now.

❖ Say the following sentences in English.
1 잘못된 것이 있는지 확인해주십시오.
2 세부 계산서를 확인해보겠습니다.
3 불편을 끼쳐서 죄송합니다.
4 계산서에서 그것들을 지금 제해드리겠습니다.

C. Complaints about the wrong room

Receptionist — Front desk. Thank you for calling. This is Dustin speaking. What can I do for you?

Guest — I just checked into room 1012. But I don't think this is my room. There are a basket of fruit and a bottle of wine on the table. I wish those were mine, but someone else's name is written on the welcome card. My name is Cindy Collins, but the name on the card is Gerald Pearson.

Receptionist — I'm really sorry for what happened, ma'am. I am afraid there must have been a mistake.

Guest — That's all right. I was just a little surprised. So what should I do now?

Receptionist — I will give you a new room. Please stay in the room until our bellman comes up to your room. As a token of our apology, allow us to give you a complimentary bottle of wine.

❖ Say the following sentences in English.
1 죄송하지만 착오가 있었던 것 같습니다.
2 사과의 표시로 저희가 무료 와인 한 병을 드리게 해주십시오.

D. Complaints about restaurant service

Guest   Excuse me. We have some problems with our meals.
Waiter   What seems to be the problem, ma'am?
Guest   I ordered my steak medium well done, but this steak is overcooked.
           In fact, it's basically burned!
Waiter   I'm terribly sorry that your steak is not cooked as you requested.
           I'll take it back to the kitchen and have the chef cook a new one.
           It will be ready in about 15 minutes. Are there any other problems, ma'am?
Guest   Yes, there is. My husband hasn't gotten his sandwich yet. Why is it taking so long?
Waiter   I'm really sorry, ma'am.
           I will check on his order with the kitchen.
Guest   Thanks. Oh, one more thing.
           Can you change my cup? It has a lipstick stain on the rim.
Waiter   I'm terribly sorry, ma'am.
           I will replace it with a clean one right away.
           (After the meal…)
Waiter   Here are some desserts for you.
           They are on the house.

❖ Say the following sentences in English.
1 어떤 문제가 있습니까?
2 저는 스테이크를 미디엄 웰던으로 주문했는데, 이 스테이크는 너무 익었어요.
3 고객님의 스테이크가 요청하신 대로 조리되지 않아 대단히 죄송합니다.
4 주방으로 다시 가져가서 주방장에게 새로 요리해달라고 하겠습니다.
5 한 15분이면 준비될 겁니다.
6 혹시 다른 문제도 있습니까?
7 주방에 주문 상태를 확인해보겠습니다.
8 가장자리에 립스틱 자국이 있어요.
9 깨끗한 컵으로 즉시 교체해드리겠습니다.
10 여기 디저트입니다. 서비스로 드리는 겁니다.

Essential Expressions | Guest Complaints

1. Apologizing to guests

I'm very (extremely/awfully/terribly) sorry for the inconvenience.
I apologize for the mistake (error).
I sincerely apologize for the experience you just had.
I'm really sorry for what happened.
I'm terribly sorry about the delay (accident/mix-up).
Please accept my apology.

2. Giving solutions to poor service

I've upgraded your room to a suite.
I will give you a new room.
I will deduct (remove) that charge from your bill.
Allow us to give you a complimentary bottle of wine.
Let me make it up to you with a complimentary bottle of champagne.
I'll take it back to the kitchen and have the chef cook it properly.
I'll bring you a new one.
I'll replace it with a new one.
I'd like to offer you a 50% discount voucher for your next stay.

Conversation II: Guest Problems

A. Guest mistakes

Operator Good evening, Ms. Wright. How may I assist you?

Guest There are some problems in my room. My kids spilled juice all over the bed.[1] In addition, they knocked a coffee cup off the table and broke it. Can you send someone to change the sheets and to clean up the broken pieces?

Operator Oh, did anyone get hurt?

Guest Fortunately, we are fine, but it is a complete mess in here.

Operator What a relief! I will report the problems to Housekeeping and have them send a room attendant up immediately.

Guest Thank you so much.

Operator My pleasure, Ms. Wright. If you need anything else, just give us a call.

Key & Alternative Expressions

1. **My kids spilled juice all over the bed.**
   = My kids dropped a glass and spilled juice on the bed.

cf. **Most common complaints from hotel guests**

Housekeeping
The toilet won't flush.
The water keeps running in the toilet.
I can't turn off the faucet.
The sink is stopped up (blocked / plugged up).
The plughole in our sink is clogged up with hair.
There isn't any soap in the bathroom.
The air conditioner in my room doesn't work.
I'm allergic to feather pillows.
The TV is out of order.
A staff member ignored the "Do Not Disturb" sign.
The room smells of smoke.

Laundry
There is still a stain on my shirt.
My scarf is faded.
My blouse is missing. It was never returned.

Front Desk
The room is too small.
This isn't the type of room I reserved.
This isn't my bill.
I've been overcharged on my bill.
There is a lot noise coming from the room next door.
A staff member was impolite.

Restaurant
This meal isn't warm enough.
This salad is too salty.
The silverware is stained.
My steak is overcooked.
The food was spilled while it was being served.
The wait staff member was inattentive.

B. Problems with room temperature 🔊 12-06

Operator   Good evening, Mr. Norman. How may I assist you?

Guest   Are you heating my room? It's too hot in here, and I can't lower the temperature.

Operator   Could you check the control box?
Please press the "OFF" button in the cooling & heating section on the control panel.

Guest   I already did that, but it made no difference.

Operator   In that case, how about turning on the air conditioner?

Guest   Where is the remote control? I can't find it.

Operator   Have you checked on the bedside table?

Guest   Yes, I did. But there was only one for TV.

Operator   You use that for everything in the room. You'll find buttons for the air conditioner at the bottom of it.

Guest   Ah, there it is. Thank you.

❖ Say the following sentences in English.
1. 객실에 지금 난방이 가동 중인가요?
2. 객실 안이 너무 더운데 온도를 낮출 수가 없어요.
3. (냉난방) 조절기를 확인해보시겠습니까?
4. 침대 옆 탁자도 확인해보셨습니까?
5. 그것을 사용해 객실 내 모든 것을 제어할 수 있습니다.

Essential Expressions | Guest Problems

1. Asking guests to check something
   Could you check the control box?
   Could you try turning it off and on again?
   Could you check if the power is on?

2. Giving solutions to problems with rooms
   I will report the problems to Housekeeping.
   I'll contact Maintenance immediately.
   I'll send someone from Maintenance to fix it.
   I'll send up a room attendant as soon as possible.
   We can change your room to another one.
   I'll have a room attendant change the sheets right away.
   I will supply it immediately.

Exercises

A Choose the best response to each question.

1. Who is responsible for fixing the facilities in guest rooms?
   a. a houseman
   b. a maintenance person
   c. a room attendant

2. Which problem is the front desk NOT in charge of handling?
   a. A nonsmoking room smells like smoke.
   b. A room is too small.
   c. The sink in the bathroom is stopped up.

3. Who delivers the new key to a guest who will change rooms?
   a. a bellman
   b. a doorman
   c. a houseman

4. If a guest room strongly smells like smoke, what most likely will the hotel staff do?
   a. try airing out the room
   b. contact Maintenance immediately
   c. move the guest to another room

B Match each sentence with the best reply.

1. There are some problems in my room.
2. I didn't expect such bad service in here.
3. Here is your bill. Please look it over.
4. Did anyone get hurt?
5. You should press the "OFF" button.

a. We are terribly sorry for the inconvenience.
b. I already did.
c. Fortunately, no one got hurt.
d. What exactly are the problems?
e. This isn't right.

C Complete the following conversation with the words in the box.

| burned | apologize | ready | token | replaced |

Guest: Excuse me. When will my burger be ¹_____?

Waiter: I'm sorry that it is taking a while. I will check with the kitchen… Here you are. Enjoy your lunch.

Guest: Wait! The patty is just ²_____!

Waiter: I ³_____ on behalf of the kitchen. I will talk to the chef and have it ⁴_____ immediately.

Waiter: Here is your hamburger. Please accept this bottle of champagne as a ⁵_____ of our apology.

Role-Playing

Make your own complaints by using each picture and practice handling them with your partner. Take turns being a hotel staff member and a guest with your partner.

Example

Receptionist : Good evening. Front desk. How may I help you?

Guest : _____.

Example

Operator : Good afternoon, ma'am. What can I do for you?

Guest : _____.

Example

Waitress : How is your meal, sir?

Guest : _____.

144 | Complaints & Problems

Looking into the Hotel — Read the following passage describes how to handle guest complaints.

Handling Complaints

No matter how hard the hotel staff tries to provide quality service for guests, it is hard to avoid customer complaints. Although no one likes receiving complaints, they give the staff members an opportunity to identify problems with their service. Complaints can also help create a bond between the staff and the customers, which can lead to customer loyalty.

There are key five steps to handling complaints properly. First, **LISTEN** carefully to a guest with an open mind. Take time to listen to what the person has to say without prejudging the situation. Maintain eye contact and let the person say everything about his or her concern. Second, **EMPATHIZE**. When listening to a complaint, try to understand how the guest feels. Put yourself in the guest's shoes, but do not make any excuses or blame others. Third, **APOLOGIZE** even if you think you have no part in the situation and you are sure that something will be done to remedy the issue. A sincere apology after a service failure can regain goodwill. Fourth, **TAKE ACTION PROMPTLY**. Try to solve a guest's problem with his or her suggested solution or an alternative you can provide as quickly as you can. In some cases, you may even need to provide a small gift to the guest to compensate him or her for the inconvenience and to thank the guest for giving you the chance to improve your service. Fifth, **FOLLOW UP**. Once you have gone through the previous steps, call the guest a week later to find out if he or she is satisfied with the solution.

Words & Phrases

blame to say that someone is responsible for a bad situation
bond a close relationship between people
compensate for to make up for
empathize to understand someone else's feelings or problems
goodwill a kind and friendly attitude toward someone or something

have no part in not to be involved in something
identify to find out what something is
prejudge to judge a situation before having enough information
put oneself in one's shoes to imagine how someone else feels in a situation
regain to get something again
remedy to correct or improve a situation

Answer Key

Answer Key

1 Switchboard

Warming Up — page 10

B a, b, d, f, g

Vocabulary — page 11

1 d 2 a 3 e 4 c
5 h 6 f 7 g 8 b

Conversation ❶ Giving Information

B. Giving information about hotel facilities — page 13
1 Thank you for calling the Lunar Hotel.
2 Does your hotel have a swimming pool?
3 The pool is located on the 5th floor inside the fitness club.
4 The pool is open from 7 A.M. until 10 P.M.

C. Giving information about hotel services I — page 13
1 How may I help you?
2 It's 15,000 won to watch one movie and 20,000 won to watch movies all day.
3 Is there anything else I can help you with?

D. Giving information about hotel services II — page 14
1 You can have breakfast at the café in the lobby.
2 The breakfast buffet is served from 5 A.M. to 10 A.M.
3 Room service is available 24 hours a day.

Conversation ❷ Handling Guest Requests

B. Connecting a guest's call to an employee in a hotel department — page 16
1 May I ask who is calling, please?
2 I'm sorry, but the line is busy.
3 Would you like to leave a message?
4 I'm afraid Mr. Lee just stepped out of the office.
5 He will probably be back by three.
6 Shall I have him call you when he returns to the office?

C. Wakeup call service — page 17
1 Good evening. Tiffany speaking. What can I do for you?
2 Could you give me a wakeup call at six tomorrow morning?
3 Good morning, Mr. Brown. This is your 6 A.M. wakeup call.
4 Have a great day.

D. Handling a wrong number — page 17
1 Mr. Chung is not a guest at this hotel.
2 I'm sorry, but there is no one here by that name.
3 What number are you calling?
4 I'm afraid you called the wrong hotel.

Exercises — page 19

A 1 a 2 b 3 b 4 c
B 1 a 2 e 3 d 4 b 5 c
C 1 speaking 2 assist
  3 connect   4 busy
  5 hold

2 Reservations

Warming Up page 22

B d

Vocabulary page 23

1 on behalf of
2 book
3 arrange
4 extra
5 guarantee
6 available

Conversation 1 — Taking Room Reservations

B. Explaining a cancelation policy page 25

1 Are there any rooms available?
2 How many nights will you be staying?
3 The rate is $250 per night, including tax and service charges.
4 What is your cancelation policy?

C. Putting a customer on the waiting list page 25

1 I'm trying to reserve a room for this weekend.
2 I'm awfully sorry, but we have no rooms available for this weekend.
3 Shall I give you the number of another hotel nearby?
4 Can you just put me on the waiting list?

D. Taking an executive floor (EFL) room reservation page 26

1 Do you have any rooms available on the executive floor?
2 It's nice to have you back, Mr. Lee.
3 Would you like to use the same credit card on file?
4 Could you give me the credit card number to guarantee the reservation?

5 You're all set.
6 Please let me know your flight number and your time of arrival.

E. Handling special requests page 27

1 How many are you in your family?
2 How old are your kids?
3 There is a $30 charge for an extra bed.

Conversation 2 — Handling Requests After Reservations

B. Changing reservations page 29

1 I'd like to change my reservation, please.
2 Let me check on that.
3 You have a reservation for a deluxe twin room for 3 nights starting on May 23.
4 I've changed that for you.

C. Canceling reservations page 30

1 I'd like to cancel a reservation, please.
2 I'm calling on behalf of Mr. David Johns.
3 Excuse me, but may I ask who is calling?
4 I've canceled his reservation.

Exercises page 31

A 1 c 2 a 3 a 4 b
B 1 e 2 a 3 c 4 b 5 d
C 1 vacancies 2 arriving
  3 staying 4 offer
  5 including

3 Door & Bell Desk

Warming Up — page 34

B b

Vocabulary — page 35

1 revolving door
2 inconvenience
3 unload
4 escort
5 spacious
6 shelf

Conversation I — Doorman Service

C. Valet parking services I — page 37

1 Where should I park my car?
2 Just leave your car here.
3 I will have someone take care of everything.

D. Valet parking services II — page 37

1 Could you get my car, please?
2 What's the plate number?
3 I'll bring your car immediately.

E. Saying farewell to a guest — page 38

1 Are you leaving now?
2 Did you enjoy your stay with us?
3 I'm pleased to hear that.
4 Do you need a taxi?
5 Here comes a taxi.
6 I'll put your luggage in the trunk.

Conversation II — Bellman Service

B. Showing a guest his or her room — page 40

1 Let me show you your room.
2 You'll get charged for what you use when you check out.
3 There are two bottles of complimentary mineral water on the shelf.
4 Our hotel has a no-tipping policy.
5 A service charge will be added to your final bill.

C. Baggage down service — page 41

1 Can you send a bellman to my room?
2 I'm checking out in 10 minutes.
3 How many bags do you have?
4 I have two suitcases and one carry-on bag.
5 I will send someone up immediately.

D. Holding baggage — page 41

1 Can my husband and I leave our bags at the hotel?
2 Let me store your luggage in our checkroom until you come back.
3 Can I have your name and room number?
4 Are these your only bags?
5 Here is your baggage claim tag.

E. Handling complaints about baggage delivery — page 42

1 I've been waiting for my bags to be sent up for almost 30 minutes!
2 I'm terribly sorry for the delay, Ms. Baker.
3 I'll check on that right away and get back to you.
4 Your bags are on the way now.
5 I'm very sorry for the inconvenience.

Exercises — page 43

A 1 c   2 b   3 b   4 c
B 1 b   2 e   3 c   4 d   5 a
C 1 way   2 After
   3 get   4 complimentary
   5 charged

Front Desk I (Reception)

Warming Up — page 46

B a

Vocabulary — page 47

1 fill out
2 lock out
3 imprint
4 extend
5 get through
6 set
7 inventory
8 closet

Conversation ① Check-In Service

B. Check-in process II — page 49
 1 May I have your business card for registration?
 2 Could you fill out this registration form?
 3 May I have your credit card to make an imprint?
 4 The bellman will take you up to your room.
 5 If you have any questions, press 0 on the room phone.

C. Checking in walk-in guests — page 49
 1 Do you have a room available for two nights?
 2 We can offer you that room at a rate of $280 a night plus tax and service charge.

D. Checking in guests with reservation problems — page 50
 1 I'm very sorry, but we don't have a reservation under that name.
 2 Do you have a confirmation number?
 3 I will check you in now, and I will confirm your reservation as soon as the Reservation Department opens tomorrow.

Conversation ② In-House Guest Service

B. Guest inquiries about a hotel shuttle service — page 52
 1 Do you provide a shuttle service for hotel guests to the downtown area?
 2 We operate a courtesy shuttle bus between the hotel and downtown every hour.
 3 The last shuttle bus leaves from the hotel at 9 P.M.

C. Assisting a locked-out guest — page 52
 1 I'm locked out of my room.
 2 Could I see some picture ID, please?

D. Guest inquiries about hotel facilities — page 53
 1 The pool and the gym are complimentary for all of our hotel guests.
 2 Where can I have breakfast?
 3 The café serves breakfast from 5:30 A.M. to 10:00 A.M.
 4 Is breakfast included in the price?
 5 Your package includes a daily breakfast for two.

E. Extending a stay & providing an extra bed — page 54
 1 Can I extend my stay for another night?
 2 Let me check if the room is available.
 3 I extended your stay one more night.
 4 Can I request an extra bed in my room?
 5 We can set one up for the additional charge of $20 per night.

Exercises — page 55

A 1 a   2 a   3 a   4 c
B 1 e   2 b   3 a   4 c   5 d
C 1 confirmation   2 booked
   3 overlooking   4 choice
   5 imprint

5
Front Desk II (Cashier)

Warming Up
page 58

B 1 credit card
   2 traveler's check
   3 bills
   4 coins

Vocabulary
page 59

1 bill
2 look it over
3 remove
4 exchange
5 mistake
6 settle

Conversation I | Checkout Service

B. Checking out a guest   page 61

1 Let me help you with that.
2 What room were you in?
3 How was your stay with us?
4 Did you use the minibar since last night?
5 It looks like you had breakfast at the café this morning.
6 Your total is 350,000 won.
7 Please look it over to see if everything is accurate.

C. Settling a bill   page 62

1 Are you using the same credit card you gave me when you checked in?
2 Can I pay with cash?
3 Your total comes to 220,000 won.
4 How much is that in U.S. dollars?
5 Here is your change. It's 20,000 won.

D. Extending the checkout   page 63

1 Let me check if the room is available first.
2 You can stay in your room until 6 P.M., but will be charged 50% of the room rate.
3 If I check out before noon, can I leave my luggage somewhere in the hotel?
4 If you need some more time to pack your luggage, I can extend your checkout around 30 minutes at no extra charge.

Conversation II | Handling Disputed Charges & Other Cashiering Services

B. Settling an account with a credit card   page 65

1 Please check it over to make sure everything is correct.
2 How would you like to pay?
3 I'm sorry, but your card was declined. Do you have another one?

C. Exchanging money   page 65

1 Today's exchange rate is 1,100 won to the dollar.
2 How much would you like to change?
3 How would you like your bills?

D. Handling guest complaints during checkout   page 66

1 Are you leaving one day earlier than expected?
2 Your room charge will be put on your company account.
3 Here is your itemized bill for the incidental charges.
4 I'll put a note in your profile.
5 I assure you it won't happen again on your next visit.

Exercises

page 67

A 1 c   2 a   3 a   4 c
B 1 c   2 a   3 d   4 b   5 e
C 1 prepare   2 number
      3 check   4 paying
      5 staying

6 Concierge & GRO Desk

Warming Up
page 70

B c

Vocabulary
page 71

1 recommend   2 try
3 on foot   4 attending
5 interested in   6 operate
7 admission fee   8 describe

Conversation I | Concierge Service

B. Recommending restaurants page 73

1 It's only a 10-minute walk from here.
2 Would you like me to make a reservation for you?

C. Locating lost items page 73

1 Can you describe what it looks like?
2 Let me get it from the back.

D. Giving advice & directions for shopping page 74

1 I need to buy some souvenirs for my family.
2 There are many street vendors at Namdaemun Market while there are many modern shopping malls at Dongaemun Market.

3 Turn left as soon as you go through hotel's revolving door, and walk straight for about 5 minutes.
4 You'll see the subway station right in front of you.

Conversation II | GRO (Guest Relations Officer) Service

B. Handling requests from a VIP guest page 76

1 Could you give me some details, please?
2 I'll need a conference room equipped with a videoconferencing system at 7:00 tomorrow morning.
3 Please make sure that there are toast, orange juice, and coffee.
4 I'll arrange a video conference for 7 o'clock tomorrow morning with five continental breakfasts.
5 Please let me know if you have any further requests.

C. Giving directions to hotel facilities page 77

1 Your conference will be held in the grand ballroom on the 2nd floor.
2 The conference is scheduled to start at 2 P.M.
3 Go straight toward the coffee shop.
4 Turn right and go to the end of the hall.
5 You can't miss it.

D. Saying farewell to a guest page 78

1 The rooms located on both ends of the corridor tend to be colder than the others.
2 I'll put a note on your profile so that you can get a room in the middle on your next visit.
3 Let me arrange a taxi and have a bellman put your baggage into the trunk while you settle the bill.

Exercises

page 79

A 1 b   2 c   3 c   4 a

B 1 a   2 e   3 b   4 c   5 d

C 1 advice   2 visit
    3 floor   4 open
    5 admission

7 Executive Floor

Warming Up
page 82

B a, b, d, f

Vocabulary
page 83

1 take a seat   2 business card
3 explain   4 all-day
5 access   6 separate
7 along with   8 billed

Conversation ① EFL Check-In & Checkout Service

B. EFL checkout service   page 85

1 Can you prepare my bill while I am having breakfast?
2 Can you make two separate bills for me?
3 I will get your limo ready and have a bellman bring your baggage down to the car.

Conversation ② Lounge & Meeting Room Service

B. EFL meeting room service   page 87

1 I'd like to reserve a meeting room, please.
2 When would you like to use it?
3 It's available at that time.
4 How many people will be using the meeting room?
5 The meeting room is available free of charge for two hours per room.
6 Can you give me another person's name?
7 If you need anything else, please contact us on the executive floor.

Exercises
page 89

A 1 b   2 a   3 c   4 b

B 1 e   2 a   3 c   4 d   5 b

C 1 hours   2 finished
    3 refreshments   4 free or charge
    5 place an order

8 Housekeeping

Warming Up
page 92

B 1 multi-adaptor   2 bandage
    3 sewing kit   4 toilet paper

Vocabulary
page 93

1 out of order   2 allergic to
3 come in   4 deliver
5 hang up   6 stain

Conversation ① Making up Rooms

B. Handling "Make up Room" service requests *page 95*
1. Can you send someone to make up my room?
2. A maid will be there right away.
3. Can you also send me an iron and ironing board?
4. I'll have a maid bring them to you.
5. That's so kind of you.

C. Handling turndown service requests *page 96*
1. I forgot to take off the "Do Not Disturb" sign.
2. Can I get turndown service now?
3. I am allergic to feathers.
4. I will send someone with a nonallergenic foam pillow right away.
5. I'll send a maintenance man to your room right away.

Conversation ② Other Housekeeping Services

B. Handling lost and found items *page 98*
1. Do you remember your check-in date?
2. What does it look like?
3. It's made of white gold, and it has a crystal pendant.
4. We are keeping it at Housekeeping.
5. A receipt and an invoice will be sent to your email.

Exercises *page 99*

A 1 a 2 a 3 b 4 b
B 1 c 2 a 3 b 4 e 5 d
C 1 Housekeeping 2 disturb
   3 make up 4 nonallergenic
   5 laundry

9 Hotel Facilities

Warming Up *page 102*
B 1 swimming pool 2 gym
   3 sauna 4 golf driving range

Vocabulary *page 103*
1 overseas 2 fragile
3 copies 4 insurance
5 rent 6 staple

Conversation ① At the Business Center

B. Printing Service *page 105*
1. If you send us the files, we can print them and deliver them to your room.
2. Your copies will be delivered within 20 minutes.

C. Courier service *page 105*
1. Please fill out this invoice.
2. Is there anything fragile inside?
3. Would you like to purchase insurance for 10 dollars?

D. Meeting room service *page 106*
1. What can I do for you today?
2. If you rent the meeting room for the entire day, you only have to pay for 6 hours.
3. You can even rent laptop computers on request.

Conversation ② At the Fitness Center

B. Swimming pool *page 108*
1. We have both indoor and outdoor swimming pools.

2 All you need to do is tell us your room number.

3 If children want to use the indoor pool, a parent or guardian should be with them.

Exercises
page 109

A 1 a 2 c 3 a 4 b
B 1 b 2 a 3 e 4 d 5 c
C 1 fitness center 2 facility
   3 indoor 4 hours
   5 change

10 Room Service

Warming Up
page 112

B 1 fried egg (sunny side up)
   2 poached egg 3 scrambled eggs
   4 boiled egg 5 omelet

Vocabulary
page 113

1 take 2 on the way
3 meal 4 boiled
5 rare 6 repeat

Conversation 1 | Taking Orders for Room Service

B. Taking an order for breakfast page 115

1 What kind of juice would you like?
2 Strawberries are in seasons now.

C. Taking an order for lunch page 115

1 How would you like your burger cooked?
2 Does it come with French fries?

3 Extra ketchup on the side, please.

D. Taking an order for dinner page 116

1 Would you like some soup or salad?
2 What would you like for dessert?
3 I am afraid it will take more than 25 minutes since we have a lot of orders right now.

Conversation 2 | Delivering Room Service

B. Handling mistakes page 118

1 Could you set up a table over there, please?
2 Let me check your order slip.
3 I will be back to pick up the service cart in an hour.

Exercises
page 119

A 1 c 2 b 3 a 4 b
B 1 c 2 a 3 b 4 e 5 d
C 1 bowl 2 come with
   3 Medium rare 4 out of
   5 in season

11 Restaurants & Bars

Warming Up
page 122

B 1 busboy 2 greeter
   3 waiter/waitress 4 bartender

Vocabulary
page 123

1 f 2 e 3 b 4 g
5 c 6 d 7 a 8 h

Conversation I — Reserving Tables & Greeting Customers

B. Assigning a table for customers with a reservation page 125

1. Under what name is it?
2. Where would you prefer to sit?
3. We have one in the corner. I will show you to your table.
4. Would you come this way, please?
5. How do you like this table?

C. Assigning a table for walk-in customers page 126

1. I'm afraid all our tables are taken.
2. Would you mind waiting until one is free?
3. Could you take a seat over there?
4. I'll call you when a table is ready.
5. I'm very sorry to have kept you waiting.

D. At the Bar page 127

1. Would you care for something to drink?
2. Would you like that straight up or on the rocks?
3. I would recommend a gin and tonic if you prefer a cocktail that isn't sweet.

Conversation II — Taking Orders & Handling Payments

B. Checking on diners page 129

1. Enjoy your meal.
2. How is everything?
3. Would you like another glass of wine?
4. Could we have another round?

C. Suggesting desserts page 129

1. I'm sorry to interrupt.
2. May I take your plates?
3. Did you enjoy your meal?
4. I'm glad you liked the food.
5. Would you like some dessert?

D. Handling payments page 130

1. We would like to split the bill.
2. A 10% service charge is included in the bill.
3. Can I have your signature and room number here, please?

Exercises page 131

A 1 b 2 a 3 a 4 a
B 1 e 2 d 3 b 4 c 5 a
C 1 dine 2 taken 3 mind 4 seat 5 show

12 Complaints & Problems

Warming Up page 134

B a, b, f, g

Vocabulary page 135

1 d 2 b 3 i 4 a 5 f
6 c 7 h 8 e 9 g 10 j

Conversation I — Guest Complaints

B. Complaints about mischarges page 138

1. Please check it over to see if there is anything wrong.
2. Let me check on the detailed bill.
3. I'm sorry for the inconvenience.
4. I will deduct them from your bill now.

C. Complaints about the wrong room page 138

1. I am afraid there must have been a mistake.
2. As a token of our apology, allow us to give you a complimentary bottle of wine.

D. Complaints about restaurant service page 139

1. What seems to be the problem?
2. I ordered my steak medium well done, but this steak is overcooked.
3. I'm terribly sorry that your steak is not cooked as you requested.
4. I'll take it back to the kitchen and have the chef cook a new one.
5. It will be ready in about 15 minutes.
6. Are there any other problems?
7. I will check on his order with the kitchen.
8. It has a lipstick stain on the rim.
9. I will replace it with a clean one right away.
10. Here are some desserts for you. They are on the house.

Conversation 11 | Guest Problems

B. Problems with room temperature page 142

1. Are you heating my room?
2. It's too hot in here, and I can't lower the temperature.
3. Could you check the control box?
4. Have you checked on the bedside table?
5. You use that for everything in the room.

Exercises page 143

A 1 b   2 c   3 a   4 c
B 1 d   2 a   3 e   4 c   5 b
C 1 ready   2 burned
   3 apologize   4 replaced
   5 token